JOE DOLCE COOKS

MY MOST LOVED RECIPES

First published by Busybird Publishing 2023

Copyright © 2023 Joe Dolce

ISBN: 978-1-922954-44-2

This work is copyright. Apart from any use permitted under the *Copyright Act 1968*, no part of this publication may be reproduced, stored in a retrieval system or transmitted in any form or by any means, electronic, mechanical, photocopying, recording or otherwise, without the prior written permission of Joe Dolce.

The information in this book is based on the author's experiences and opinions. The author and publisher disclaim responsibility for any adverse consequences, which may result from use of the information contained herein. Permission to use any external content has been sought by the author. Any breaches will be rectified in further editions of the book.

Front and back cover Images: Dolce family archives

Layout and typesetting: Busybird Publishing

Photography, musical score illustrations and poetry: Joe Dolce

Artistic Design & photographic post production: Kev Howlett

Paintings and front cover photo: Lin van Hek

Busybird Publishing
2/118 Para Road
Montmorency, Victoria
Australia 3094
www.busybird.com.au

Dedicated to Blaise van Hecke
without whom this book would not have been made

> *Cooking is a little rascal; it often leads to despair.*
> Pellegrino Artusi

Every culture has its dishes that give nostalgic or sentimental value. This is the food that is traditionally associated with the security of childhood. The terms: *mama's cooking* or *grandma's cooking*. These dishes can be different for different people, even within the same household.

This food was usually prepared by traditional housewives long before the trend of male celebrity chefs.

My own personal comfort food comes from memories of my Sicilian grandmother, 'Little Grandma', preparing our weekly feast at her house. She cooked down in her basement kitchen, a dark mysterious corner, with a steel-doored, coal-fired furnace on one side and a cold room for storing canned root vegetables from the garden on the other.

Our extended family gathered, every Sunday afternoon, to sit at the big round dining table on the floor above where she laboured. She only came up the stairs to serve the never-ending array of recipes that she, in turn, learned from her own mother and grandmothers.

For me, prime comfort food was spaghetti and meatballs. But other dishes of hers that I remember were braciola (meat rolls), stuffed with provolone or pancetta, and her home-made bread, baked in the upstairs second oven.

> Six white loaves rising,
> amber through the burnt oven glass,
> out the tic-tac-toe
> kitchen window,
> grandpa bends over,
> swearing in Italian at tomato bugs.

The tomato sauce (*sucu*) was home-made from tomatoes harvested from their large back garden. (I mean large! It took three women to do the bottling.) And grandma's garden was *nothing* compared to her father's garden who lived a couple of suburbs over in a poorer neighbourhood, next to the railroad tracks. 'Big Grandpa', as we referred to him had a home garden the size of an entire field, complete with chicken coop and shed for making home-made wine. He'd often lock himself inside when we came to visit. I remember my grandmother, banging on the shed door and cursing at him, in Sicilian slang, to come out and spend time with his great-grandchildren!

My 'little' grandma was a master pastry chef and her antique side table would always be filled with cookies, biscuits, candies and cakes she would prepare for the family. Her skin smelled of almonds and vanilla. One of her own Sicilian sisters, who was no slouch at cooking, once remarked to me: 'your grandmother was a *genius* cook.'

The collection of recipes in this book is not strictly traditional Italian-American.

I've always had a good ear, musically, able to work out popular songs by just listening to records.

In a similar way, I have a good aptitude for figuring out the ingredients of the dishes I like - especially if there was no way to experience those dishes again.

I had to learn how to make them myself if I was ever going to eat them again.

Also, once my grandmother passed away, this was the *only* way I could get close to the food I grew up eating.

I suspect that this is the way many cooks began cooking - from the absence of something that is missed so much in their lives, they have to recreate it back into existence.

In the fifty or so years I have been cooking, primarily for my family, I have collected way too many recipes to commit to memory so I depend on written-down notes. If you are cooking pretty much the same selection of dishes week after week, year after year, decade after decade, as our mothers and grandmothers did, sooner or later, you naturally commit them to memory.

But, like musicians playing an international cornucopia of classical music, if your repertoire includes many different masters from many different cultures and times, then a well-notated score, or, in our case, a well-notated recipe, is essential. The dishes you tend to make most often will be the ones that you learn by heart. Others, you might only eat once or twice a year, if that, and it's easy to forget one key ingredient, or the *order of ingredients*, that often defines the dish.

Our mothers and grandmothers learned everything they know from *their* mentors – the older women in their families. Instead of looking at a recipe, they looked at their mama. If she smiled, you knew you got it right; if you got it wrong, you got – well, best case, the 'stare'- and worst case, a wooden spaghetti spoon across your behind.

Apprentice chefs follow the written-down instructions of master chefs who create the ever-changing menus - even in Michelin-starred restaurants.

So there's no shame in following recipes. It's logical and natural. Like Salvatore Dali once said, 'If you are afraid to imitate, you will create nothing.'

I have chosen to focus this cookbook on the food I prepare regularly. A few are my original ideas, always constructed, of course, on the foundation of the many cooks and recipes that have come before and have inspired me. There are often only one or two dishes from each cuisine, but they are the ones I look forward to making and eating. Each dish in this book is a 'love' recipe.

One of the most recent brilliancies I discovered is the Indonesian *Sop Buntut* (Oxtail Soup) which I ran across in Bali - one of the great nutritious bone broths of the world, along with Jewish Chicken Soup and Vietnamese Phở.

Most of these recipes have precise measurements but many don't. As my brother's Italian mother-in-law, Rose, once told him when he asked her how much basil to add to a dish: 'Just PUT IT IN!'

You learn cooking primarily by cooking.

Try whatever interests you here, from my rough instructions, and take your own notes. If something doesn't taste the way you like it, add more or less of something. As my Balinese cooking instructor once told me, 'if it doesn't taste right, add more palm sugar'!

I trust you will enjoy and fall in love with some of these dishes – and the cultures, and people, that created them – as I have over the years.

Joe Dolce, Carlton North, VIC, Australia 2023

The pasta spoon

I attribute my unerring sense of rhythm,
the accuracy at which I am able to play,
dead on beat, to my mother's skill,
with the pasta spoon.

Bent over her aproned lap,
for one digression or another,
she brought the heavy wooden baton
down onto my backside,
like a skilled German conductor.

I – told – you – not – to – do - that

One word per strike, metrical,
marrying forever, pain, and precision,
word and rhythm.

Don't – ev - er - let – me - catch - you – do - ing – that - a – gain

Short, sharp, per - cuss - ive, Protestant words.

I was blessed she never knew the value
of a thesaurus.

Contents

L'APPETITO vien mangiando. (Eating awakens the appetite.) — 1

Truffle Popcorn	2
Roast Chestnuts w/ Chestnut Pesto	4
Chestnut Hummus	4
Don Diego's accordion (poem)	6
Don Diego's Jalapeño Poppers	8
Chipolte Corn-On-The-Cob	12
Chipotles in Adobo Sauce	14
Mixed Olives & Olive Oil	15
Sweet-Salty Chili Peanutsw/Kari Leaves	16
Ligurian Olive & Basil Pesto w/ Red Chili	18

Buone come il PANE. (Good as bread.) — 21

Pancetta, Field Mushroom & Mozzarella Pizza	22
Breakfast Rolls	24
Joe's Fried Bread	24
Chapatis	24
Art of Focaccia	26
Easy No-Knead Baked Bread	28
Iraqi-style Gözleme-Böreka	30
Yogurt-Garlic Sauce	31
Turkish Gözleme	32

Tutte fa BRODE. Everything makes broth.) — 35

Stinging Nettle & Potato Soup	36
Stinging Nettle Chapatis	38
Chicken Soup w/Kneidlach(matzo balls)	39
Feather-light Matzo Balls (Kneidlach)	40
Tomato Soup	42
Sop Buntut	44
Congee	46
Chive Crème Fraîche	48
Conjuring phở (poem)	49
Phở Bò	50
Boat people (lyrics)	54
Nước Chấm / Nước Mấm	56
Phở Bò Pie	58
Perilla Nốc Mấm Pha Dressing	61
Bún Chả	62
French Onion Soup	66

Fare POLPETTE di qualcumo. (To make meatballs of someone) — 69

Grandma's Spaghetti & Meatballs	70
Meatballs Stuffed w/Mozzarella	72
Tomato-Vodka-Cream Accelerator Sauce	72

'e Fusilloni, w/ Guanciale, Basil-Chili Tomato Sauce, Fennel Sausage & Kangaroo Braciole — 74
Four Peppercorns — 78
Trafilata al Bronzo Fusilli — 80
Tagliatelle Puttanesque! — 81
Strascinate di Cascia — 82
Nuit étoilée — 84
Grilled Eggplant Slices — 85
Eggplant Parmesan — 86
Aphrodite's Magic Girdle Moussaka — 88
Knife penny (poem) — 90

Cosa bolle in PENTOLA? (What's boiling in the pot?) — 93

New England Corned Beef & Cabbage Boiled Dinner — 94
Lin's Hot Paprika Goulash — 96
Osso Buco Milanese-Style — 100
Irish Lamb Stew — 102
Lamb Shanks w/ Mashed Potatoes — 104
Ethiopian Leg of Lamb — 106
Eric's Steak — 108
Breaded Veal Schnitzels — 110
Veal Muscat Dolce — 112
Sweet Potatoes w/ Ginger: — 113
Green Beans w/ Almonds: — 113
BBQ Spareribs — 114
Red-eye Gravy BBQ Sauce Accelerator — 116
Brown Sugar, Maple Syrup & Cinnamon Glazed Ham — 117
Roast Pork w/ Crackle & Gravy — 118
Smothered Pork Chops — 120
Pig tails in gravy (lyrics) — 123
Ragout des Pattes de Porc — 126
Sausages & Jalapeños — 127
The rime of the ancient gooney bird (poem) — 129
Salt Sarcophagus Chicken — 130
La Mama's Lost Lebanese BBQ Chicken w/ Lemon & Garlic — 132
Ode to a baccalà (poem) — 134
Baccalà Vesuvio — 136
Baccalà, Flamed Tiger Prawns & Fennel Aglio e Olio w/ Spaghettini — 138
Chiles en Nogada — 140
Satan's Claws Christmas Baccalà w/ Red Jalapeño Peppers & Green Sicilian Olives — 144
Risotto di Zucca — 148
Grapefruit Risotto — 150
Risotto Con Funghi in Flagrante Delicto — 152
Risi e Pisi con Finocchio Liberace — 154
Arancini — 156
Sweet Potato Gnocchi — 158
Polenta — 160
Nasi Tumpeng w/ Satays & Choko-Chicken Kari — 162
Balinese Choko-Chicken Kari — 164
Beef & Chicken Satays — 166

Cashew Nut Kari	168
Potato Kari	170
Green Cabbage Kari	172
Watermelon, Spinach & Feta Salad	174
North Vietnamese Kohlrabi Salad	176
Potato & Pumpkin Salad	178
Peace & Love Salad	180

Più — 183

Fried Green Tomatoes, w/Guanciale	184
Egg Foo Yung	186
Sausage Gravy	187
Flemish-style Tossed Potatoes w/ Dill	188
Cookbooks for poets (poem)	189
Eggs Obstáculos	190
Poached Eggs in Milk on Toast w/Nutmeg	192
Eggs-Over-Easy	192
Lemonscent (poem)	194
Annie's Preserved Lemons	195
Nastro Azzurro Fried Onion Rings	196
Roast Garlic Hummus	198
Elegy for old feller (poem)	200
Breaded Silverbeet Stalks	201
Chile Rellenos	202

DOLCE e con affetto — 205

Inzuppare il biscotto (poem)	206
Kama Sutra Chocolate Tart	208
Lemon Curd Cheesecake	210
Pineapple Upside-Down Cake	212
Kahlua Pecan Pie	214
Good karma pudding (poem)	216
Wintermoon Persimmon Pie	217
Mexican Peanut Butter Pie	220
Lemon Tart	222
Mille Foglie	224
Raspberry Coulis	225
Clafoutis	226

Essere la ciliegina sulla TORTE. (To be the icing on the cake.) — 229

Red Velvet Cake (lyrics)	230
Red Velvet Gold Coin & Snake Cake	232
Red Velvet Cake w/Cherries	234

acknowledgements	236
about the author	239

Truffle Popcorn

INGREDIENTS
½ cup salted butter
black truffle shavings or fine gratings
popcorn

METHOD

- Pop the popcorn in the regular way in a little oil in a pot with a lid.
- Make sure you lift the lid now and then to let the steam out or the popcorn will be soggy.
- Remove the popcorn and melt the butter in the same hot pot, off the heat.
- Finely grate or shave some truffle into the butter.
- Stir and pour over the popcorn.
- Finely grate or shave a little truffle over the top and add a little salt and black pepper, if you like, but not too much or you will overpower the truffle flavor which is sublime.

Roast Chestnuts w/ Chestnut Pesto

INGREDIENTS

chestnuts, some for eating and some for the pesto
fresh basil
garlic
cold pressed olive oil, walnut oil or flaxseed oil

METHOD

≡ Roast the chestnuts over a fire or in a hot oven (approx. 45 minutes). Peel. Combine a couple handfuls of peeled nuts with some garlic, fresh basil leaves and a little salt into a mortar and pestle. Pound until smooth and reduced. Add some oil. Pound some more. Correct the taste as you like it. Place a couple of tbsp of pesto on a plate with the roasted chestnuts.

Chestnut Hummus

INGREDIENTS

fresh chestnuts
flaxseed oil
garlic, chopped finely
salt
lemon
paprika

METHOD

≡ Cut an X in each chestnut with a sharp knife. Boil them in water for 30 minutes. Allow to cool. Cut each chestnut in half and scoop the flesh out with a small teaspoon. Mash the chestnut meat with flaxseed oil and garlic until a smooth dip is achieved. Salt to taste. Drizzle some flaxseed oil over the top with an optional squeeze of lemon or a little paprika. Serve with toasted ciabatta, and fresh carrot, cucumber and celery sticks.

Don Diego's accordion

I quit childhood accordion lessons
due to a time conflict with Zorro
my favourite b&w tv show of the 50s
three slashes of sword
whishhht! whishhht! whishhht!
like the sign of the cross
cut a Z into many young hearts
I hung up the rapier and bullwhip
shortly after George W Bush was run
out of town on the back of El Toro
but occasionally don the black cape and mask
to help local townspeople
with corrupt politicians and greedy landowners
and for infrequent shopping mall appearances
Zorro Spanish for fox pronounced *soro*
credited with inspiration
by their respective creators
for The Lone Ranger and Batman
whereas the accordion inspired
the blind and the file
I think I made the right choice.

Don Diego's Jalapeño Poppers

INGREDIENTS

1 dozen fresh, firm jalapeños
240 g cream cheese, softened
240 g sharp cheddar cheese, grated coarsely
panko bread crumbs
flour
2-3 beaten eggs
crisp bacon, pancetta or guanciale, chopped finely (optional)
oil for deep-frying

METHOD

- Slit the jalapeños carefully half-way across the cap, being careful not to detach it, and long ways down the middle making a T-cut. Carefully separate the edges and spoon out the seeds and membrane.

- Mix the cream cheese and the cheddar cheese together. (Bacon, pancetta or guanciale can be fried, crumbled and added to the cheese mixture.) Stuff into the cavities of the jalapeños. Dip in flour, then egg wash, then bread crumbs. Place in the fridge until ready to deep-fry.

- Deep-fry in hot oil until golden.

- Serve warm.

Stuffed Jalapeño Popper Mouse

METHOD

- Add some sliced red bird's eye chili ears and a couple of black peppercorn eyes!

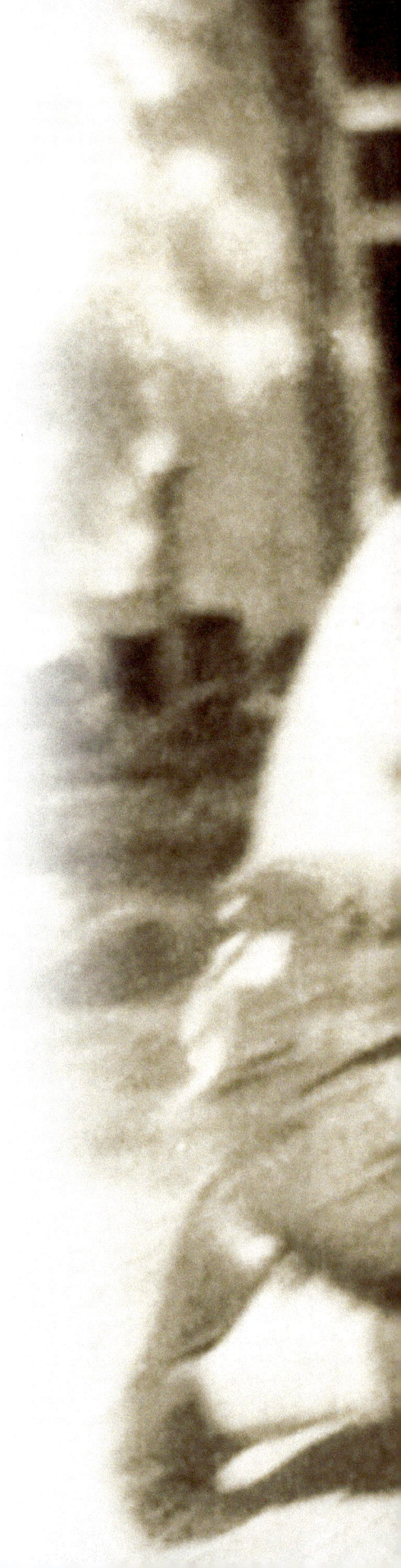

Here's a little boy and his father
kissing a single ear of corn
between them.
No hands.

The man's shirt off,
the lean and muscular body
and permed hair I recognize.
He could make a bicep
the size of a softball.
I don't recognize the boy
but grandma says that it's me.

Chipolte Corn-On-The-Cob

Traditional Mexican street-stall fare.

INGREDIENTS
4 ears corn, shucked
1 dried chipotle chile
¼ cup melted butter
½ cup mayonnaise
½ cup grated hard feta cheese (or grated parmesan or cotija cheese)
4 wedges lime
cayenne pepper

chipotle mayonnaise:

METHOD

- Take one dried chipotle chili and fry in oil until it turns colour. Drain on paper towel and cut open, removing and discarding the seeds. Tear the chili into pieces and soak in hot water for a half hour until soft. Put the chili pieces into a blender with a couple of tablespoons of the soaking water. Blend into a paste. Mix into the mayonnaise. Season with a little salt.

- Preheat an outdoor grill, or stove top grill-pan, to medium-high heat. Boil corn in hot water until half cooked. Grill corn until hot and lightly charred all over.

- Roll the corn in melted butter, then spread evenly with chipotle mayonnaise. Roll again in grated cheese and sprinkle with cayenne pepper. Serve with a cayenne pepper-sprinkled lime wedge.

Tip: Try substituting Chipotle mayonnaise in dishes that use regular mayonnaise e.g. potato salad, bacon, lettuce and tomato sandwiches, devilled eggs, fish and chips, hamburgers, etc.

Chipotles in Adobo Sauce

'This is a handy way to prepare the chipoltes in advance.'

INGREDIENTS

7 to 10 medium-sized dried chipotle chiles, stemmed and split lengthwise
⅓ cup onion, cut in ½ inch slices
5 tablespoons cider vinegar
2 cloves garlic, sliced
¼ cup ketchup
¼ teaspoon Salt

METHOD

- Combine all of the ingredients in a pan with 3 cups of water. Cover and cook over very low heat for 1 to 1 ½ hours, until the chilies are very soft and the liquid has been reduced to 1 cup. This recipe will keep for several weeks in the refrigerator in an airtight container.

Mixed Olives & Olive Oil
w/ Rosemary, Garlic & Orange Peel

INGREDIENTS

1 cup of plain or mixed olives: jumbo queens, Ligurian, dry blacks
10 fillets of unsalted anchovy, in oil
olive oil
1 sprig of rosemary
3 unpeeled cloves of garlic
1 tbsp of fresh orange peeled zest
1 red bird's eye chili, whole
balsamic vinegar

METHOD

- Use flat unsalted white anchovies in oil rather than the rolled salted brown ones in jars and tins.

- Heat about a ½ cup of olive oil in a fry pan.

- Add the orange peel and sauté for two minutes.

- Add the rosemary sprig, the garlic, bird's eye chili and the mixed olives.

- Sauté until rosemary is crisp, careful not to burn the garlic and until the olives are puckered. On a serving plate, lay out the anchovies on one side and on the other place the olives. Put the rosemary sprig on top of the olives, scatter the garlic around and spoon some of the hot oil and orange peel over the top. Shake a couple drops of balsamic vinegar onto the olives (just a bit, not too much).

- Serve with crusty bread as an appetizer.

Sweet-Salty Chili Peanuts w/Kari Leaves

INGREDIENTS

300 g salted peanuts (or almonds)
140 g caster sugar (more, if required)
2 tbsp oil
1 tbsp water
handful fresh kari leaves
2 tsp sea salt flakes
2 tsp sliced fresh bird's eye chili

METHOD

- Place peanuts and sugar in frying pan over medium heat.
- Add scant 1 tbsp of water (not too much!) and stir to combine.
- Cook, stirring, for two minutes until sugar begins to coat the peanuts and water evaporate.
- Reduce heat and cook, stirring for 10 minutes, or until some of sugar begins to caramelise. If it starts smoking remove from heat, but continue cooking for another ten minutes until nuts are crystalized and candied.

If the nuts look too wet, add more sugar until a dry crystalized texture is achieved. (Be careful not to over-cook or you will end up with peanut brittle! Which isn't a bad thing, but that's not what we're making!)

- Cool on baking paper.
- Wipe out pan, add oil and set over medium heat.
- Add kari leaves and sauté for 30 seconds until fragrant and crispy but do not burn.
- Drain on paper towels.
- Add sliced chillies to pan for two minutes.
- Drain.
- Add leaves and chillies to nuts and transfer candied peanuts to serving bowl.
- Toss through with sea salt.

Ligurian Olive & Basil Pesto w/ Red Chili

INGREDIENTS

fresh basil
½ cup small Ligurian black olives, without the pits
pine nuts
2 cloves garlic, chopped finely
cold pressed olive oil
freshly grated parmesan cheese
½ red chili, seeded and chopped finely
salt and freshly ground black pepper

METHOD

- Chop fresh basil roughly. Put the basil leaves, garlic, red chili, pine nuts and salt into a mortar and pestle.
- Pound until reduced to paste.
- Add chopped olives, parmesan cheese and black pepper. Pound until smooth.
- Add some olive oil.
- Pound some more. Put aside in dish or a jar with a tight fitting lid.
- Flatten pesto in the dish or jar and cover with a layer of olive oil to keep out oxygen.
- Cover dish with plastic wrap and put in the fridge until required. Serve with any kind of pasta, risotto or polenta.

Also nice on toasted ciabatta or dry biscuits.

Buone come il PANE.

(Good as bread.)

Pancetta, Field Mushroom & Mozzarella Pizza

INGREDIENTS

basic pizza dough (recipe below)
2 large field mushrooms, sliced thinly
8 thin slices of pancetta
large ball of wet mozzarella, pulled apart into threads.
fresh roquette leaves (arugula)
a little tomato passata
olive oil
chili flakes
green Sicilian olives, pitted and sliced (optional)
parmesan cheese, grated

You don't need a swish pizza oven to make great pizza. Improvise with what you have. I often make pizza, in the bush, in a camp oven over an open fire.

METHOD

- Place oven rack in the middle to avoid burning the bottom. A pizza stone is handy.
- Gradually stretch out dough until required size. Do not roll. Place it on a pizza tray and continue to pull and tug gently. Don't worry about sections that are a bit thin – they will crisp up and be crunchy. Allow to rest and rise further for a half hour.
- Heat oven to highest temperature.
- Spread a thin layer of passata over the dough and place the mozzarella around it. Scatter sliced mushrooms, olives (if using) and pancetta around pizza. Sprinkle a little Parmesan and red chili flakes. Drizzle a little olive oil over the top. Bake for about 10-15 minutes. Watch it carefully. If the bottom cooks too fast, move it to a higher rack. If the top cooks faster than the bottom, move it to a lower rack.
- Add some fresh roquette for a garnish.

♪ nOte: This can also be made without tomato passata.

The Crust

I never use measurements when I make pizza. But I definitely encourage you to follow recipes - until you have an intuitive feel for the dish.

I usually just throw some flour in a bowl, sprinkle in some dried yeast and salt, stir, and put the bowl under the warm water tap, stirring, until it starts to come together.

There's an old saying, 'Anything worth doing, is worth doing poorly. Poorly can always be made better.' So, in this case, as we say in the recording business, 'we'll fix it in the mix' - i.e. if the dough is too dry, add more water. If it's too wet, add more flour.

INGREDIENTS
2 cups of flour
1 tsp salt
1 tsp dried yeast
1 tsp bread improver (optional)
a cup or two of warm water

METHOD

- Put the flour, salt, dried yeast and bread improver in a bowl and mix thoroughly. Heat the water to just warm (baby bottle temperature) and gradually stir into the mixture a little at a time. Watch the consistency. You want the dough a little wetter than you usually have it for standard rolling.

The stickier and lighter the dough, the easier it is for the yeast to rise it. There are no mistakes here. Each different consistency results in a different kind of crust. I like light and airy loaves with lots of air bubbles and a crunchy crust so I make my dough a little stickier. Don't worry. It all comes out right in the end! Trial and error. Once the dough comes away from the bowl and is the consistency you like, cover with a cloth for an hour.

- After the first rise, remove the cloth and stir well with a wooden spoon. Turn the dough onto a floured board, cut into balls (for each pizza), gently stretch and pull to approx. a disc of 1-inch thick, and allow to rise for another hour. You can spoon a little olive oil over the top to keep it from drying out.
- A half hour before you are ready to bake, preheat the oven to the hottest temperature. Place the dough onto the pizza pan and gently pull and stretch again, using your fingertips to make it a bit thinner. *Do not roll with rolling pin!* Allow to rise for the time it takes the oven to reach very hot.
- Add ingredients and bake for ten-fifteen minutes or until crust is the way you want it. Watch that the bottom doesn't burn. Move to a higher rack if necessary.

Breakfast Rolls

Break off a few sections of the above dough, form into small rounds, fold over itself and gently flatten. Let rest for 20 minutes. Stretch gently and put a very hot oven for ten minutes. If you're lucky, and it puffs up, break into pieces and toast or serve hot from the oven. Great for breakfast or to serve with dinner.

Joe's Fried Bread

This is one of Lin's favourites. Take a few sections of the above dough and roll out into a small oval patty. Let rise for about a half hour while you are washing your face in the morning. Heat up a skillet with olive oil and fry the bread until golden on both sides. Drain on paper towels. Serve with butter and jam.

Chapatis

This is basically the pizza dough – without the yeast. Just mix flour, water and salt together and let rest for fifteen minutes Roll them out flat and either bake in a hot oven for ten minutes or cook on the stove top in a dry frying pan. Black pepper, sesame seeds or garlic can be added for variety.

Art of Focaccia

INGREDIENTS
500 g 00 flour
7 g dried yeast
325 ml warm water
salt
2 tbsp olive oil
decorative herbs, vegetables and edible flowers of your choice, including mushrooms, capsicums, asparagus, a variety of tomatoes, fresh rosemary and sage.

This is a labour-of-love focaccia. I made the base and Lin van Hek decorated it.

METHOD

- Mix flour, yeast, water and salt in bowl.
- Stir with a spoon. Flour your hands and knead for ten minutes. (This stretches the gluten.) Cover bowl for 40 minutes. (This creates some humidity and 'proves' the dough.)
- Sprinkle some coarse polenta or semolina on a baking tray.
- Lay dough on tray and spread it with your fingers to stretch. Spread olive oil over the stretched dough and poke indentations all over with your fingers.
- Decorate.

♪nOte: oil all the fresh herbs before placing on dough.

- Cover with warm wet towel for 45 minutes until double in size.
- Preheat oven to 200°.
- Sprinkle salt and pepper over dough.
- Bake for 20-25 minutes.
- Remove from oven and 'feed' with more olive oil.
- Cool for ten minutes.

Easy No-Knead Baked Bread

INGREDIENTS

3 cups of flour
1 tsp salt
1 tsp dried yeast
1 tsp bread improver (optional)
a cup or two of warm water
sesame seeds
Dutch oven, with a lid
a little water
rectangular bread tin, to fit inside Dutch oven
strip of newspaper, baking paper or aluminium foil, about two-inches wide and three feet long, folded over into thirds to make a kind of long paper 'strap' to lift the bread tin into the Dutch oven.

If you want to get two for the price of one, make an extra quantity of this dough and keep some of it aside, for a pizza the next day. The dough is pretty much the same as for the pizza, with the added rising time required for bread. However, you can break off a section of the dough, before it rises, and stick it in the fridge for tomorrow's pizza. The cold will slow down the rise and in the morning, take it out and pull it into an approximate circular shape. Let it go through another rising process.

I neither measure ingredients precisely when I make bread nor do I knead the dough. I only stir it with a wooden spoon and pull it. It always comes out perfectly. Here is the technique I learned from making sourdough, by using a Dutch oven and a bread tin.

METHOD

- Pre-oil lightly the rectangular bread tin.

- Put the flour, salt, dried yeast and bread improver (if using) in a bowl and mix thoroughly. Heat the water to just warm (baby bottle temperature) and gradually stir into the mixture a little at a time. Watch the consistency. You want the dough a little wetter than you usually have it for standard rolling. The stickier and lighter the dough, the easier it is for the yeast to rise it. Each different consistency results in a different kind of loaf. Once the dough comes away from the bowl and is the consistency you like, cover with a cloth for an hour.

- After the first rise, remove the cloth and stir well with a wooden spoon. Turn the dough into the bread tin and allow to rise for another hour. You can spoon a little olive oil over the top to keep it from drying out or else just place a towel over it.

- A half hour before you are ready to bake, preheat the oven to hottest temperature and place the Dutch oven and the lid inside. You want the Dutch oven HOT!

- After the dough has fully risen, (do not let it fall), carefully sprinkle sesame seeds over the top and then slip the paper 'strap' under the bread tin so that you can use it to lift the tin.

- Remove the Dutch oven, and the lid, with two mitts or towels, being careful not to burn yourself, and set it on the stovetop. Gently lift the bread tin with the strap and place it into the Dutch oven. Using a knife or chopstick, slowly and gently lift the edge of the tin a little and slip the paper strap out, then tip a little water into the Dutch oven, on the side of the bread tin (not in it!), for steam and quickly place the lid on the oven. Steam should be coming out of the sides. Place the Dutch oven back into the main oven and close the door. Set the timer for fifteen minutes. After fifteen minutes, remove the lid and check the bread. It should be golden and about half done. Leave the lid off and continue baking for another 10-15 minutes. The timing of these two parts is flexible depending on the heat of the oven and the size of the loaf. Sometimes the first bake practically finishes the bread. Other times, you only need ten minutes for the second bake. The first bake cooks the interior and the second bake generally crisps up the outside. Carefully remove the loaf from the Dutch oven and turn onto a wire rack. It should come easily out of its pan as well. I suggest eating a slice of the end immediately with butter and letting the rest cool down before further cutting. There is nothing like that first slice straight out of the oven, dripping with melted butter!

Iraqi-style Gözleme-Börek

INGREDIENTS
3 cups of flour
1 tsp salt
1 tsp dried yeast
1 tsp bread improver (optional)
a cup or two of warm water

Böreks traditionally use filo pastry and gözleme dough doesn't have yeast. This recipe walks the line between both of them. The bread roll is made using the basic no-knead recipe above, but with one difference: stretching and folding the dough between rises.

METHOD

- Put the flour, salt, dried yeast and bread improver (if using) in a bowl and mix thoroughly. Warm the water (baby bottle milk temperature) and gradually stir into the mixture, a little at a time. Watch the consistency. You want the dough a little wetter than you usually have it for standard rolling. The stickier and lighter the dough, the easier it is for the yeast to rise. Once the dough comes away from the bowl with the consistency you like, leave the spoon in and cover with a cloth for an hour. After the first rise, remove the cloth and pull the bread, from one end, into the air. Fold it over itself on all four sides and place on a floured surface. Lightly push it down and pat it together with your hands into a round ball. Cover with plastic wrap and leave to rise again for an hour.

- Turn the dough onto a floured board, shape and cut into pieces for each börek. Stretch it with your fingers and shape into a flat thin parcel long enough to allow you to fold it in half over the top of the ingredients. Let it rise for another half hour. Now it's ready to add the ingredients.

INGREDIENTS

1 bunch of silverbeets, steamed and finely chopped
1 onion, finely chopped
feta cheese, crumbled
salt and pepper
1 egg

METHOD

- Preheat the oven to hot.

- Sauté the onion in a little oil and season with salt and pepper. Set aside. Cut the tough part off the silverbeets. Wash and spin dry.

- Steam until soft. Chop finely. Cool. Mix with the onion and the egg. Spoon the mixture over one-half of the rolled out dough and break up the feta cheese and sprinkle over the top. Be generous with the ingredients! Fold the dough over and seal the edges, pressing down firmly as flat as possible without breaking the surface. Brush some water across the surface of the dough and bake in the oven for 10-15 minutes. The longer they stay in the oven, the crispier the outside crust so if you like your crust soft, take them out earlier. Serve with Yogurt-Garlic Sauce.

Yogurt-Garlic Sauce

- Mash two cloves of garlic (more if you like it stronger) with some salt in a mortar and pestle. Add the yogurt, a squeeze of lemon juice and a little olive oil and mix well. Put in a bowl, cover with plastic wrap and refrigerate until ready to serve.

Turkish Gözleme
Anatolian flat bread

I learned this one by watching some Turkish women make it in a tent at a festival in Jamberoo.

for the dough:

INGREDIENTS
120 g strong unbleached flour
½ tsp salt
1 tbsp olive oil or melted butter
60-90 ml lukewarm water

for the filling:

feta cheese, crumbled finely
silverbeet leaves, with the stems and veins removed,
torn into one-inch pieces

METHOD

- Sift the flour with the salt into a bowl. Make a hollow in the middle and pour in the oil and water using your hands to draw flour in from the sides.

- Work the mixture into a dough and knead well. Divide it into 4 pieces and roll into balls. Place on a floured surface, cover with a damp cloth, and leave to rest for 20 minutes.

- Roll the balls of dough into thin flat rectangular shapes, approx. 30 cm x 20 cm.

- Place a fine layer of cheese on one-half of the rectangle, sprinkle some silverbeet pieces over, and fold in half. Press flat and seal the edges with a little water.

- Heat the griddle, wipe it with oil, and place one of the rectangles on it. Use your fingers to shift the dough about, making sure it browns and buckles. About a minute or two. When the first side is done, flip it over and cook the other side.

- Place on a board, cut into 2-inch squares with a sharp knife and squeeze fresh lemon juice over the top. Eat while hot. Serve with some large queen-sized olives on the side.

♪ nOte: you can also fill it with sautéed finely chopped onions, browned minced beef or lamb, or add some freshly sliced mushrooms.

Stinging Nettle & Potato Soup

Another ingredient I never knew existed until Lin alerted me to it. Stinging Nettle grows wild all over our NSW bush property but nobody in the area eats it because they are wary of the painful stingers on the leaves. But it is child's-play to blanch and remove these and what you are left with is an incredibly nutritious, and free, wild vegetable, that can be used for cooking and also makes a brilliant fertilizer for the garden. You can even smoke the dried leaves!

To prepare the nettles:

Destem the nettles (wearing gloves) and parboil the leaves for 30 seconds. This will remove the stingers. Try one to test! (Better you than your guests!) You can test it by rubbing some on your wrist. 30-seconds is more than enough time to de-sting them. You also don't want them too squishy. Strain and place in cold water to stop them from cooking. Chop finely.

For the potato soup:

INGREDIENTS

olive oil
2 potatoes, chopped finely
1 stalk of celery, chopped finely
1 clove garlic, chopped finely
1 onion, chopped finely
chicken or vegetable stock
salt and pepper

METHOD

- Place a little oil in a deep pot and sauté the onions and celery until soft.
- Add the garlic and stir for a minute.
- Add the potatoes and stir.
- Add the stock. Cook for 20 minutes or longer depending how firm you want the vegetables.
- Add the cooked chopped nettles, salt and pepper and heat up for a couple minute.
- Serve with sour cream.

Stinging Nettle Chapatis
This basically uses the pizza/bread dough recipe.

METHOD

- Mix the flour, water, dried yeast and salt together and let rest for fifteen minutes.
- Destem the nettles (wearing gloves) and parboil the leaves for 30 seconds.
- Chop finely and mix into the dough.
- Roll the chapatis out flat into round shapes and either bake in a hot oven for ten minutes or cook on the stove top in a dry frying pan.
- Black pepper, sesame seeds or garlic can be added for variations.

Chicken Soup w/Kneidlach (matzo balls)

Chicken soup has been called 'Jewish penicillin' for hundreds of years and recent nutritional research agrees. Professional athletes are becoming advocates. Sports nutritionist, Dr Cate Shanahan said:

The traditional approach is based on the idea that chefs were the original nutritionists. Everything they would naturally do—use things in season, use the whole part of food, pay attention to source—has nutritional benefits.

Before it shut its doors, I made many trips to the iconic Russian-Jewish restaurant, Scheherazade, in St Kilda, on Wednesdays (the only day they made matzo balls) and humbled myself before the masters. It had been years since I tasted a great chicken soup with kneidlach and - just like returning to classic literature for writing inspiration - once again I was reminded of the important and easily forgotten 'Zen of Matzo' principles, such as lightness (melt-in-your-mouth, not chewy) clarity and colour (clarified and lightly saffroned stock) and crucial seasoning (fresh dill). I immediately went home and fine-tuned my own recipe (which, truth be told, was getting a bit lead-footed in the matzo.) Here it is. Only for serious chicken soup fans who are prepared to put in the time and care to get the results (or want to relieve cold symptoms!)

♪nOte: taking extra time to prepare the stock as a bone broth (24 hours of simmering) enhances flavour and healing attributes.

Bone Broth differs from stock only in the amount of time you simmer the bones. Up to 24 hours if you have the patience. The bone marrow is fully absorbed into the broth. Rich in amino acids, which help prevent inflammation in the digestive track, it is easy to digest, and comes in handy when you are ill and are having trouble eating salads and other vegetables. It is said to walk the line between food and medicine.

INGREDIENTS
1-2 chicken carcasses (bones)
2 chicken breasts
bay leaf
some black pepper corns
the whites of 4 eggs
half-finely chopped onion
half-finely chopped carrot
a piece of muslin

a handful of uncooked white rice.
four or five strands of good saffron
a couple of tbsp of lemon juice
salt to taste

day before: METHOD
- Make the chicken stock. Place chicken carcasses (bones) and chicken breasts in a pot of water (about two inches above the chicken pieces), add bay leaf, and black pepper corns. Bring to a boil, skim off as much of the scum from the top, reduce heat to a simmer and cook for about an hour. (For a bone broth, simmer for 12 or more hours, adding water, if needed.) Put in fridge overnight.

next day:
- Spoon off about a half cup of 'smaltz' (chicken fat) and stock to use for the matzo balls. Strain the stock, shred the chicken pieces slightly and set aside.

to clarify the stock:
- Place the egg whites, finely chopped onion and carrot into a blender and blend until frothy. Pour the mixture into the stock and bring to a low simmer and simmer for about a forty minutes. A 'raft' of debris will form. Strain the stock carefully through a piece of muslin, watching not to disturb the 'raft' in the centre. Place the clarified stock into a clean pot, add the chicken pieces and uncooked rice.
- Add the saffron to the lemon juice and a couple tablespoons of hot stock and stir well. Let rest for about fifteen minutes until the golden colour is released from the saffron. Stir into the stock. Add salt to taste.

Feather-light Matzo Balls (Kneidlach)

INGREDIENTS
3 cups fine matzo cracker meal, or matzo crackers, or (as a last resort) any saltine biscuits.
5-6 eggs, beaten
a few drops of water
2 tbsp of smaltz (chicken fat)
salt

Matzo meal is hard to find and so are matzo crackers. If you are using whole crackers, place them in a plastic bag, and jump on them, waving your hands in the air ecstatically, until they are all smashed up. Or put them in a mortar and pestle, or blender. Get them into a fine cracker meal any way you can. Place them in a bowl. Add the beaten eggs. Add the melted smaltz. (This is a key ingredient to the flavour and the 'magic healing properties' - don't ask me why, just do it! - I get my smaltz when I make a chicken stock, I leave the stock in the fridge overnight. In the morning, the fat rises to the surface. Skim it off and save it for the matzo balls.) - Add the few drops of water. Stir well and leave to sit for half hour.

The trickiest part to making matzo balls is getting them light enough. This is trial and error. Thomas Edison once said, 'I didn't just invent the light bulb; I first invented 99,000 ways how *not* to invent the lightbulb'. You have to find your own way here. If the mix is too wet, they will fall apart when you put them in the hot water. If the mix is too solid and firm, they will be as dense as Joshua's Goitre. You have to get them light enough to just hold together so they keep their shape without falling apart. Light, so a fork passes through them easily. (Corrective surgery: If the mix is too wet, add a bit more cracker meal. If the mix is too solid, add a little more water. Mix again and let set for another 20 minutes or so.) When you get it right, you'll know it. The blind will be able to see again, the deaf: hear; the afflicted: restored, and the lame . . . well, unfortunately, it doesn't work for the lame - they still be draggin'.

When the mixture has firmed up, and the cracker meal has absorbed the eggs, wet your hands and form into small balls - golf ball size - and drop into a pot of rapidly boiling water. Cover the pot and reduce to a simmer. Simmer gently for about a half hour. Prepare the matzo balls separately from the soup in clean boiling water, and THEN add them to the simmering soup. Cover the pot and let the balls absorb soup flavours for about half hour.

Tomato Soup
w/Mountain Pepper Berry, Kneidlach & Chive Crème Fraîche

(A vegetarian variation of the preceding dish)

INGREDIENTS

4 cups fresh ripe tomatoes, chopped
4 cups water
1 onion, finely chopped
1 tbsp sugar
fresh basil
olive oil
ghee
salt to taste
Mountain Pepper Berries, finely ground in a mortar and pestle
matzo balls (kneidlach), as in previous recipe

METHOD

- Place some olive oil and ghee in a pot and heat until smoking.
- Add onions and sauté until clear.
- Add tomatoes, sugar, salt and some chopped fresh basil.
- Cook for five minutes. Add water. Bring to a boil, cover the pot and reduce the heat to a simmer. Cook until tomatoes have broken down - about an hour.
- Put the contents of the pot into a blender and blend for 2 minutes. Return to the pot and reheat.
- Add Mountain Pepper Berries and salt to taste.
- Place two kneidlach in a bowl, cover with tomato soup.
- Sprinkle some finely ground Mountain Pepper Berry, (as you would black pepper), a dollop of crème fraîche and chives, and a couple sprigs of fresh basil to finish.

Sop Buntut
(Indonesian oxtail soup)

I discovered this recipe accidentally in Bali. I had been staying in inexpensive pensione-type local accommodation and came down with a severe respiratory problem. We transferred over to a 4-star hotel, on the beach, with a good staff doctor who put me on a portable respirator for an afternoon which solved the problem. On the hotel menu was Sop Buntut. I was curious and ordered it. It was the best dish I have ever had in Bali.

INGREDIENTS
1 kg oxtail pieces
2 ½ litres water
2 tbsp olive oil
1 cinnamon stick
5 cloves
1 tsp nutmeg
2 medium carrots (peeled and cut into half-inch pieces)
2 medium potatoes, (peeled and cut into 6-8 wedges)
1 tbsp salt
1 tsp black pepper
1 tbsp sugar

paste:

10 shallots
5 cloves garlic
1-inch piece of ginger

garnish:

12 cherry tomatoes, halved
1 scallion, cut into thin slices diagonally
2 pieces of celery, peeled and thinly sliced
1-2 limes (in wedges)

Kepac Manis-chili sauce:

4 tbsp Kepac Manis
1 red bird's eye chili, seeded and sliced

day before:

Boil oxtails and water in large saucepan. Simmer for 3 hours on low heat until oxtails are tender. Remove oxtails from broth and set aside. Strain stock. Return oxtails to pot. Cool and put in fridge overnight.

METHOD

on the day:

- In the morning, spoon off the thin layer of fat on the surface and set aside (for excellent piecrusts e.g. Oxtail Pie!)
- Reheat the stock and oxtails.
- Grind the paste in a mortar and pestle.
- Heat oil and sauté the paste in frying pan until fragrant. Add cinnamon, cloves and nutmeg. Stir five minutes. Add to the main pot with the broth and oxtails.
- Bring to boil. Add carrot and potato and season with salt, pepper and sugar. Lower heat and cook 20 minutes until vegetables are cooked but firm.
- Serve soup with fresh halved cherry tomatoes, green onions and celery. Serve steamed rice on the side, with the chili sauce and fresh limes.

Congee

The primo Asian breakfast comfort food. An excellent use for left-over rice.

rice:

INGREDIENTS
1 cup white rice, washed
4 cups water

METHOD

Make rice in advance. Add the rice to the water, in a very large pot. Cover, bring to a boil, reduce to lowest heat and cook for about half hour. The rice won't fully absorb the water but that's ok.

Cook slowly for about an hour, watching it occasionally, adding more water as necessary. The consistency we are looking for is a soupy porridge, where the rice breaks down, but not as thin as soup. (You need to have eaten congee once to know what it should look like.)

garnishes:

Lap chung (dried Chinese sausage), finely sliced, on the diagonal. Steam in a small covered bamboo steamer, or gently fry over low heat until fat is released. Set aside.

Any Asian greens (fresh), washed and cut into one inch pieces. Steam for a minute, or cook gently in a little water. Keep firm. Do not overcook. Set aside.

Arrange some small garnish dishes of deep fried shallots, or onions, shoyu, or light soy sauce, fresh coriander, stems off, and fresh red chillies, finely sliced.

Place the congee in a bowl, with some soy sauce, sliced red chillies, chopped asian greens, a handful of steamed lap chung sausages, and fresh coriander. Sprinkle some fried shallots over the top and serve, with extra shallots, chillies and soy sauce on the side.

Chive Crème Fraîche

INGREDIENTS

chives, chopped finely
crème fraiche

METHOD

≡ Add the chives to the crème fraîche (or sour cream).

♪nOte: crème fraîche has two advantages over sour cream: it can be whipped like whipping cream, and it will not curdle if boiled.

Conjuring phở

Boiled clean beef ribs
pile-stacked like
xylophone wood
industrial sized pot-au-feu
balancing on point
single pre-Indochina War gas jet
bubbling brown bath at first glance
more dishwater-dressed than stock
miraculously grandmother transformed
into a bowl of richest broth
sea dragon cellophane rice noodles
verdant flecked chives white baby
spring onion sliced red chile squeezed
lime fragrant star anise
Hanoi street alchemy
priceless at two dollars.

Phở Bò

I first discovered this dish in early 1980 when I was living in small flat in Richmond, Victoria. The arrival of the Vietnamese 'Boat People' in Darwin was in the daily news. I had written and produced a recording, of a protest song I had written, *Boat People*, but I had never met any actual Vietnamese people.

I was walking down Victoria St and saw the only Vietnamese restaurant in Melbourne, at the time, Vào Đời (New Beginning). I looked through the front window and saw little playschool-type tables, with a thermos bottle on each one and small stools. There was only one dish on the menu. Phở: for $2. Out of curiosity, I went in. The combination of soup with salad greens was so unusual and addictive that I came back every day for lunch!

Eventually I made friends with the cook, Hung, who had been an activist and doctor in South Vietnam until his family was forced to leave. He couldn't practice medicine in Australia so he turned to cooking. One day, I brought in a hundred 45 rpm recordings of my *Boat People* record and asked Hung to distribute them amongst the new arrivals as 'welcome to Australia' gifts. He liked my song and invited me to his house for dinner and to meet his family. I asked him if I could bring anything. He said to bring some ingredients and make them a home-made pizza! We spent the night singing Vietnamese and American folk songs. They knew dozens of sad songs filling with longing and loss of country.

Phở is the well-known Vietnamese *national* comfort food and can be made with any type of rice noodle. The Hmong people, north of Hanoi, use thick hand-made noodles.

INGREDIENTS
1 kg rice noodles (bánh phở)
1 kg brisket bones
400 g beef rump or brisket
150 g beef eye fillet, finely sliced
20 g shallots
30 g old ginger
3 pieces star anise
3 cm piece cinnamon stick
1-2 tbsp black cardamon seeds
1 lime or lemon
100 g spring onions
3 litres of water
salt and pepper

small square of muslin cloth and string, to tie
fresh herbs: mint, coriander, saw coriander, basil.
mung bean sprouts
½ red or yellow onion, or combination of both.
fish sauce (Nước Chấm/Nước Mắm)
fresh red chilli
finely minced fresh ginger

METHOD

- Make the broth in advance. (The day before.) Prepare the fresh herbs an hour or so before serving. Prepare the noodles and beef eye fillet immediately before serving.
- Wash the bones and meat.
- Grill the ginger and the shallots. Set aside.
- Lightly roast the cardamom seeds, the star anise and the cinnamon stick. Be careful of the star anise as it burns quickly. You might want to remove the star anise and the cardamom seeds after about 30 seconds and let the cinnamon stick stay a little longer.
- Crush the roasted spices roughly in a mortar and pestle, combine with the grilled ginger and shallots, place in the square of muslin and tie securely with the string. (If you plan on straining the stock, it is not necessary to make a sachet – just put the spices directly into the pot.)
- Place 3 litres of cold water in a pot and put in the bones. Turn heat up high and when the water boils, skim. Place the spice sachet and beef brisket or rump in the pot. (The raw beef fillet is saved until serving time). Season with a little fish sauce and salt, and simmer, covered, on low heat for about two and a half hours. Take the spice sachet out when the stock has become fragrant, after about two hours. Take out the meat, drain well, cover with plastic wrap and set aside. If you want to make a bone broth, keep simmering for another two hours on low heat, adding a little more water if necessary. Take out the bones and discard.
- Let the stock cool and refrigerate until the next day.
- In the morning, lift the solidified fat off the stock and discard (or reserve for Phở Bò Pie!) Slice the uncooked beef fillet very thinly, place in a small bowl and marinate in the finely minced ginger. Set aside until ready. Wash the fresh herbs and place side by side, with the bean shoots, on a large serving dish. Slice the spring onion (diagonally) and finely slice the onion. Soak the dry noodles in warm water for 15 minutes. Blanch the noodles in boiling water for about 5 minutes until al dente, and quickly refresh in cold water. Place some noodles in each bowl, with some spring onions, onions, and some sliced cooked beef. Pour on the boiling stock. Place the uncooked ginger-marinated eye fillet slices in a ladle and poach in the simmering stock for a few seconds and then add some to each bowl.
- Serve immediately accompanied by cut lemons and limes, sliced red chillies, the fresh basil, mint and corianders, bean shoots, Nước Chấm/Nước Mắm, chili sauce and kecap manis.
- Tip: Ice water is the friend of freshly-cut herbs.

Boat people

Boat People come from an old country,
sail across dangerous seas,
nomad people all through history,
pilgrims, slaves, convicts and refugees

We are the Boat People one and all,
we are the Boat People hear the call,
pilgrims, slaves, convicts and refugees,
are the sum of all humanity,
we are the Boat People.

Boat People perish at sea
death becomes their avenue to liberty
while councils convene to hear their pleas
with hearts grown numb from luxuries

Boat People come to a strange new land
it's customs they're struggling to understand
while in the course of their integration
they meet violent discrimination.

We are the Boat People one and all,
we are the Boat People hear the call,
pilgrims, slaves, convicts and refugees,
are the sum of all humanity,
we are the Boat People.

Words & Music: Joe Dolce 1979.

(Vietnamese translation: David Huynh.)

THUYỀN NHÂN (Những Người Vượt Biển)

Thuyền nhân đến từ những nước cổ xưa
Vượt Đại dương đầy nguy hiểm
Những người lang thang trong lịch sử:
Tha phương, nô lệ và tị nạn.

Chúng ta đều là những thuyền nhân
Chúng ta đều nghe những tiếng gọi:
Tha phương, nô lệ và tị nạn
Tất cả đều là nhân loại.
Chúng ta là những thuyền nhân.

Thuyền nhân mất nơi biển cả,
Sự chết trở thành con đường đi tới tự-do.
Nhân loại đều nghe tiếng kêu gào của họ
Với những con tim tê tái từ sự đau khổ.

Chúng ta đều là những thuyền nhân
Chúng ta đều nghe những tiếng gọi:
Tha phương, nô lệ và tị nạn
Tất cả đều là nhân loại.
Chúng ta là những thuyền nhân.

Thuyền nhân đến một vùng đất mới lạ.
Họ phải đương đầu với một tập quán mới.
Trên con đường đi tới sự hòa hợp,
Họ gặp bao trở ngại và chông gai.

Chúng ta đều là những thuyền nhân
Chúng ta đều nghe những tiếng gọi:
Tha phương, nô lệ và tị nạn
Tất cả đều là nhân loại.
Chúng ta là những thuyền nhân.

Nước Chấm/Nước Mấm
This is basically the Vietnamese 'salt and pepper'.

INGREDIENTS
1 cup hot water
3 tbsp caster sugar
2-3 tbsp fish sauce (to taste)
2-3 tbsp apple cider or white vinegar (to taste)
1 tbsp lime juice
1 fresh red bird's eye chili, sliced
1 clove garlic, minced
½ stalk of lemongrass (cut in slices, white part only)
1 tbsp finely shredded carrot
a thin slice of lime or lemon

METHOD

- In a medium sized bowl, dissolve the sugar in the hot water. Add the fish sauce, vinegar, garlic, lime and lemongrass and chillies, mixing until thoroughly combined. Let rest for at least one hour.

- Before serving, add shredded carrot and the slice of lime or lemon.

Phở Bò Pie
w/ Chili Tomato Sauce & Vietnamese Salad

top crust:

INGREDIENTS

sheet of puff pastry

METHOD

- Roll out and cut into a circle large enough to cover pie pan.
- Set aside until ready.
- 1 egg, beaten for wash.

bottom crust:

INGREDIENTS

2 parts phở lard (lifted from the top of freshly made phở stock, strained and left over night in refrigerator).
3 parts flour
salt

METHOD

- Mix ingredients together until dough holds together. Wrap in plastic wrap and put in refrigerator for fifteen minutes.
- Preheat oven to 200°C. Oil pie pan or pans. Roll dough into ⅛ inch sheet large enough to cover the pie pan. Press down into the pan and trim edges. Prick surface with a fork to prevent bubbling. Cover with baking paper and weights (dried beans, etc) and blind-bake for ten minutes. Remove paper and weights and bake for a further 8 minutes. Watch it and adjust time to suit your oven. Do not over-bake. Pat down any pastry that has puffed during cooking. Set aside to cool.
- Increase oven temperature to 220°C.

filling:

INGREDIENTS

300 g cooked phở brisket, enough to fill pie pans, chopped finely
100 g fresh eye fillet, cut into small chunks
2 tbsp plain flour
60 ml vegetable oil
1 medium brown onion, roughly chopped
1 small celery stick, thickly sliced
310 ml good-quality phở stock
2 tbsp fresh parsley, finely chopped
½ tsp salt
freshly cracked black pepper

METHOD

- To make filling, place finely chopped brisket in bowl. Set aside. Place chopped eye fillet in another bowl, add flour and toss to coat. Heat half of oil in a medium heavy-based frying pan over medium-high heat. Add fillet and cook, using a wooden spoon to stir often, for 6 minutes or until light brown. Transfer to a bowl. Reduce heat to medium. Add remaining oil to pan. Add onion and celery, and cook, stirring, for 2 minutes. Return eye fillet and chopped brisket meat to pan with phở stock, parsley, salt and pepper. Bring to a simmer over medium-high heat. Reduce heat to low, cover and simmer for 30 minutes, or until beef is tender. Increase heat to medium and cook, uncovered, for a further 10 minutes or until sauce is a thick gravy. Taste and adjust seasoning with salt and pepper. Transfer filling to a bowl and set aside for 15 minutes to partially cool.

- Spread cooled filling evenly onto pastry base until even with top edge or slightly above. Use a pastry brush to lightly brush pie edge with a little cold water. Place puff pastry on top of pie and gently press edges together to seal. (Do not press the outer edge too hard, or it will not puff well during baking.)

- Poke top of puff pastry with a fork to allow steam to escape during cooking. Lightly brush top with beaten egg. Place pie on baking tray and bake in oven for 15 minutes. Reduce oven to 190°C and cook for a further 20-25 minutes or until well puffed, golden and heated through. Keep an eye on it – baking time may be less if oven is especially hot. If necessary, shield areas of pastry top and edges browning faster than others with pieces of foil. Serve immediately.

sauce:

INGREDIENTS
tomato sauce
Thai sweet chili sauce
1 green or red chili, chopped finely.

- Mix ingredients together and put in small bowl.

salad:

A selection of fresh phở salad herbs: mung bean sprouts, chives, coriander, Vietnamese mint, basil and shredded lettuce.

- Wash, spin and place in serving bowl.

Perilla Nớc Mấm Pha Dressing

INGREDIENTS

1 cup hot water
5 tbsp sugar
2 tbsp fish sauce
1 small garlic clove, minced
2 ½ tbsp vinegar (and/or fresh lime juice)
½ tsp finely sliced fresh red chili peppers
1 tbsp finely shredded carrot
1 perilla leaf, (tía tô), finely shredded.

METHOD

- In a medium-sized bowl, dissolve the sugar in the hot water.
- Add the fish sauce, vinegar, garlic, perilla leaf and chili, mixing thoroughly.
- Cool.
- Add shredded carrots.
- Dress the salad leaves and serve.

Bún Chả

Bún Chả is the signature street-dish of Hanoi, much as phở is for the South. It is not as common to find this dish in Australia but it is the equal to phở in flavour and healthful ingredients (bone broth and fresh herbs).

The overview for this dish is: thin slices of marinated and grilled pork belly and 'meatballs', in a sweet pork broth, with herbs and rice noodles. The signature herb is perilla leaf (tía tô). Locate this before you even consider making this dish because this single herb is what gives the recipe its unique character.

marinade for meat:

INGREDIENTS

10 spring onions (scallions), thinly sliced
100 g chives and/or garlic chives, roughly chopped
6 tbsp minced red Asian shallots
12 cloves garlic, minced (4 tablespoons)
1 tsp freshly ground black pepper
4 tbsp fish sauce
4 tsp dark soy sauce
5 tbsp honey
500 g minced pork
500 g pork belly, finely sliced
1 egg, lightly beaten
500 g rice vermicelli noodles, cooked
1 bunch perilla leaves, plucked
1 bunch fresh Asian basil leaves, plucked
1 bunch fresh Vietnamese mint leaves, plucked
1 bunch fresh mint leaves, plucked
1 bunch chives and/or garlic chives
some finely shredded mixed small lettuce leaves

pickled papaya:

INGREDIENTS

½ small green papaya
Ratio of marinade: 1 vinegar: 2 sugar: 2 water

METHOD

- Thinly slice papaya (1 cm).
- Make enough marinade to cover the surface. Leave to rest at room temperature for at least 2 hrs.

table condiments:

INGREDIENTS

1 small red bird's eye chilli, diced
1 clove garlic, diced
1 lime, quartered

night before:

METHOD

- Make the marinade. In a mixing bowl, combine the spring onions, garlic chives, shallots, garlic, black pepper, fish sauce, honey and soy sauce.
- In separate bowl, combine half the marinade, minced pork, and egg and mix well.
- Add the sliced pork belly to the remaining marinade. Cover and marinate both meats in the refrigerator for 2 hours, or overnight for a better result.
- Make pork broth by simmering some pork bones, or some of the pork mince, for about 20 minutes. (As an option to grilling the meat patties, you could also roll them into meatballs, simmer in the broth and add to the finished strained soup when you serve.
- Cool stock. Strain and put in fridge overnight.

on the day:

- Skim the fat off the top of the broth, add the ingredients for the dipping sauce/soup broth.

Dipping sauce or soup broth:

INGREDIENTS

Ratio: 1 sugar: 1¼ vinegar: 1 fish sauce: 10 pork broth.
Example: for 540 ml broth, enough for 4 people, you will need: 40 ml sugar: 50 ml vinegar: 40 ml fish sauce: 400 ml water or pork stock.

METHOD

- In a medium saucepan, combine all the ingredients above and cook over low heat until the broth is lukewarm.
- Cook the rice vermicelli in boiling water for about 12 minutes. Drain and plunge in cold water twice. Drain and cut into manageable pieces with scissors. Place in a bowl on the table.
- Cut the herbs and lettuce leaves with scissors until manageable size. Place in a bowl on table. Place the condiments in a small dish on table.
- Heat a charcoal grill or barbecue to medium hot.
- Form the pork mixture into small round balls with oiled hands, then slightly press down on each ball to form patties, about 2 inches/5cm in diameter and ½ inch/1cm thick and grill the patties for 4 minutes on each side. Set aside.
- Grill the pork belly slices for 2 minutes on each side. Set aside.
- In each serving bowl, place some chopped chives or garlic chives, the two kinds of meat and some sliced pickled papaya. Add broth to cover. Put the remainder of the meat on a platter and set on the table.

to serve:

- Add a mixture of noodles, herbs and meat into the warm broth.
- Have separate bowls of each of the ingredients on the table so you can add more of anything.

French Onion Soup

INGREDIENTS

½ kg yellow onions, cut into ⅛ inch pieces
3 tbsp unsalted butter
½ tsp table salt, plus more as needed
1 pinch sugar
8 cups water, plus more as needed
1 tbsp all-purpose flour
1 sprig fresh thyme (save some for finish)
¼ cup dry white wine
1 baguette, crusty
8 ounces Gruyère cheese, thickly sliced and placed over the top of the crock. The cheese melts mostly into the soup and a little off to the sides and creates a thick, even layer.

METHOD

- Melt butter in a large Dutch oven or soup pot over medium heat. Add the onions, ½ teaspoon salt, and sugar. Toss to evenly coat. Cover and cook for 10 minutes.

- Take the cover off, and cook, stirring frequently, until the onions are lightly browned. I cooked mine for a little less than 90 minutes. Stir every 5 minutes and add water (a tbsp at a time to loosen up the dark brown stuff that forms on the bottom of the pan). Continue to cook until the onions are an even dark brown colour, an additional 30 minutes longer or so.
- 'Add the flour and stir for two minutes. Add 8 cups water and thyme to the onions and bring to a boil. Lower heat and simmer for 20 minutes. Add white wine and simmer 10 minutes longer. Add salt to taste.
- Meanwhile, heat the oven to 165°C and adjust a rack to the upper middle position. Cut the baguette into ¾ inch slices and arrange on a single layer on a cookie sheet. Bake until the bread is dry, about 10 minutes.
- Remove bread slices and set aside. Heat broiler and place 6 heatproof bowls in a baking sheet. Fill each bowl with about 2 cups soup.
- Top each with two baguette slices and evenly distribute cheese slices over the bread. Sprinkle over some fresh thyme.
- Put bowls under broiler until well browned and bubbly, about ten minutes. Cool for five minutes before serving.

Fare POLPETTE di qualcumo.
(To make meatballs of someone.)

Grandma's Spaghetti & Meatballs

This dish is comfort food for just about every Italian in the world. I make the meatballs separately, as my grandmother did, and mound them up in a bowl. Then I add them to the already simmering sauce which itself is chock full of other meats. For serving, I separate the meats from the sauce and serve the meat in a separate bowl.

for the meatballs:

INGREDIENTS

250 g ground beef
250 g ground lean pork
1 egg
fresh breadcrumbs
finely chopped garlic
finely chopped onion
finely chopped parsley
some white wine
salt & pepper
olive oil, for frying

METHOD

- Mix all ingredients together well. Form into balls, small or medium, as you like. Fry in the oil until cooked through. The fresh breadcrumbs keep the meatballs light. (Just like matzo balls, you don't want them too dense.) Eat them as they are, in sandwiches, or else, as for this recipe, simmer them in the tomato sauce.

for the sauce:

INGREDIENTS

Italian fennel sausages
beef or pork back ribs
carcass of a chicken, cut into segments
plain tomato passata, with no added herbs or spices - except possibly basil
olive oil
garlic, chopped
1 onion, finely chopped
1 chicken stock cube, dissolved in a cup of warm water
fresh basil leaves
salt, pepper & sugar
½ red bird's eye chili
parsley, finely chopped

METHOD

- Fry the sausages in some oil. Remove from pan. Brown the chicken carcass segments. Remove from pan. Add the onions to the pan and cook until soft. Add the garlic and red chili. Stir for a minute. Add some white wine and cook for a couple of minutes. Add the passata, meats, chicken carcass, stock cube, herbs and spices. Cook for an hour, stirring occasionally. Add the meatballs. Keep simmering until ready to serve.

- Discard the chicken bones, and remove the sausages, ribs and meatballs to a separate bowl. Strain the sauce.

for the pasta:

- Cook some spaghetti in boiling salted water, until al dente. Remove about a cup of pasta water and reserve. Drain the pasta and put back in the pot. Spoon about a half-cup of the sauce over the pasta and stir well. Add about a half-cup of the reserved starchy pasta water to help bind the sauce and pasta together. Serve on a plate, with a nice spoon of sauce over the top (not too much), with grated parmesan, fresh ground black pepper, chopped parsley and a little drizzle of olive oil. Serve the meats in a separate bowl or else put a couple of meatballs on each mound of pasta.

Meatballs Stuffed w/Mozzarella

As a variation, you can place a small cube of mozzarella cheese in the centre of each meatball before frying.

Tomato-Vodka-Cream Accelerator Sauce

I read somewhere that this was one of actress Michelle Pfeiffer's favourite ways to prepare a pasta sauce.

Very simple.

METHOD
- Heat up the pasta sauce of your choice. (I use a basic pomodoro sauce.)
- Add ⅓ vodka.
- Cook for a few minutes to evaporate the alcohol.
- Add ⅓ cream.
- Heat up and serve.

You can also add chopped pancetta, fresh basil or chili flakes to give it more depth. Use a strong vodka.

'e Fusilloni, w/Guanciale, Basil-Chili Tomato Sauce, Fennel Sausage & Kangaroo Braciole

Winner of the Non-Professional Category: Great Pasta Sauce Competition, Hepburn Springs Swiss-Italian Festa 2007.

Braciole are thin slices of meat pork, chicken, or beef, rolled with cheese and bread crumbs and fried. In Italy, they are also called Involtini. (It is also a slang term in Italian for the male organ, but don't let that put you off.) I've always liked to use indigenous Australian ingredients when I could think of something creative. I once made dried cod (baccalà) with Murray River cod.

In this one, I've used kangaroo. Someone once said that Australians are the only country in the world that eat the animals on their National Coat-of-Arms!

'e fusilloni is a very large corkscrew pasta.

for the sauce:

INGREDIENTS
best quality olive oil
1 anchovy
1 small diced yellow onion
¼ inch slice of guanciale (cured pig's cheek)
wings and back of chicken
2 tsp finely chopped garlic
¼ teas red chilli flakes
1 cup dry white wine
2 litres tomato passata (buy a simple one containing only tomatoes and water - no herbs and spices - or make your own)
1 bay leaf
1 tbsp sugar
½ teas freshly ground black pepper
handful fresh basil leaves
salt
six Italian fennel pork sausages (buy them or make your own)

for the kangaroo braciola:

4 thin boneless kangaroo cutlets, cut and pounded thinly into a flat rectangular schnitzel shape for rolling (ask the butcher to do this for you and then give them a few extra whacks yourself at home before preparation.)
4 thin slices of ham off the bone
4 thin slices of salami (remove rind)

4 thin slices of prosciutto
4 thin slices of soppresata (remove rind)
4 thin slices of provolone cheese
cooked ground Italian fennel sausage meat (removed from casing)
fresh garlic, chopped
fresh parsley, finely chopped
freshly ground black pepper
grated Romano or parmesan cheese
strong black thread or kitchen string for tying
500 g 'e fusilloni pasta

METHOD

- Gently lay out the thin pounded slices of kangaroo fillets. Season meat with garlic, black pepper, and parsley. Layer slices of all meats and provolone in the centre. Add ground sausage and sprinkle with the grated cheese. Fold in the two sides of meat. Roll up the meat, keeping all ingredients inside. (Practice makes perfect.) Secure and tie with string.

- Brown the chicken pieces briefly in some olive oil. Remove from pan and set aside. In the same oil, brown the fennel sausages until just cooked. Remove from pan and set aside. In the same oil, gently brown all sides of the kangaroo braciole. Remove and set aside. Scrape the brown bits from the bottom of the pan into the oil and reserve.

- Heat quarter cup fresh olive oil in deep skillet. Add a quarter-inch thick slice of guanciale. Add one whole anchovy and mash into oil until dissolved. When the guanciale begins to release its fat, add one small finely chopped onion. Cook slowly allowing the onion to release its flavour and become translucent. Add the garlic and red chilli flakes. Cook for a minute watching CAREFULLY that the garlic does not burn. (Yuck! If you lose focus and the garlic burns, throw everything out and start over from scratch with a fresh pan). Add the white wine and reduce by half. Add the tomato passata, bay leaf, sugar, black pepper and the chicken pieces. A little salt. (Be temperate with the salt at this stage as the braciole and fennel sausages are salty and the parmesan cheese, to finish, also adds some salt. Fine tune flavouring later before serving).

- To the simmering sauce, add the fennel sausages, the kangaroo braciola rolls and some of the oil that the meats were browned in (a couple tablespoons for added flavour). Cover and simmer over very low heat for an hour or two. Make sure the sauce does not thicken too much. If it does, add a little chicken stock or water.

- When the chicken is practically falling off the bone, remove the braciola and the sausages and set aside. Strain the sauce through a coarse sieve or colander. Pick out the chicken bits and remove any usable meat from the bones and set aside. Discard bones. Pick out basil leaves and set aside. Strain the sauce again through a medium sieve so that it has a smooth texture. Place sauce in a clean pot with the chicken bits, the basil, the fennel sausages and the braciola rolls. Return to the simmer and cook for a further 15 minutes.

- Cook the pasta until al dente. Remove about a cup of pasta water and reserve. Remove the braciola rolls and gently discard the threads. Slice into half-inch slices. Start from the centre and try to keep the shapes intact. Place some sauce in a frying pan, bring to a simmer and toss spaghetti, or penne, in the sauce until lightly coated (do not do the heavy red sauce number!). Add about half cup of starchy pasta water to help bind the sauce to the pasta. Serve the sauce-coated pasta on a plate with a fennel sausage and a couple slices of braciole, freshly grated parmesan cheese and some chopped fresh parsley.

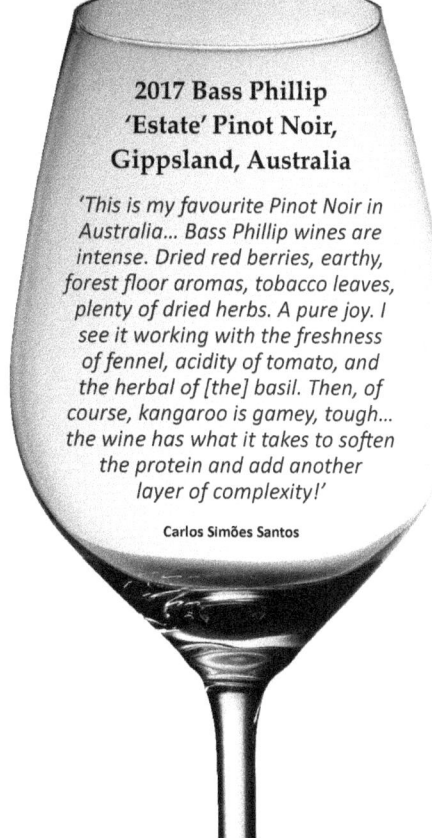

2017 Bass Phillip 'Estate' Pinot Noir, Gippsland, Australia

'This is my favourite Pinot Noir in Australia... Bass Phillip wines are intense. Dried red berries, earthy, forest floor aromas, tobacco leaves, plenty of dried herbs. A pure joy. I see it working with the freshness of fennel, acidity of tomato, and the herbal of [the] basil. Then, of course, kangaroo is gamey, tough... the wine has what it takes to soften the protein and add another layer of complexity!'

Carlos Simões Santos

Four Peppercorns

A simple recipe with a few ingredients and a lot of surprises.
I serve it with a side of lightly pureed silverbeet.

INGREDIENTS
1 tsp each of red, white and black peppercorns.
1 tsp of whole marinated green peppercorns, drained
2 tbsp of olive oil
25 g of butter
500 g spaghettini
chopped parsley
parmesan cheese

METHOD

- Place red, white and black peppercorns in a mortar and pestle and grind semi-finely. Reserve in a small bowl.
- Place green peppercorns in another little bowl.
- Heat 2 tbsp of olive oil and 25 g of butter in a pan.
- Add half of each of the bowls of peppercorns and mix well.
- Bring water to boil.
- Cook the pasta al dente and drain.
- Add pasta to serving bowl and stir in the peppercorn sauce.
- Sprinkle over the reserved wet and dry ground peppercorns.
- Add some grated parmesan and chopped parsley.

Trafilata al Bronzo Fusilli
w/ Italian Sausage, Chestnuts & Sautéed Beet Greens

INGREDIENTS

3 links of Italian sausage (preferably fennel & pork)
pine nuts, toasted
small-medium greens from 4 beets
large clove of garlic
olive oil
½ fresh red chili, chopped
20 fresh chestnuts
parmesan cheese, grated
parsley, finely chopped
salt and pepper
500 g pasta

METHOD

- Cut an X in the flat side of each chestnut, boil in some water for 10 minutes, and peel, one at a time, leaving the remainder in the water. The chestnuts are easier to peel if they are hot. Peel the outer skin and as much of the inner brown skin as you can. Set aside.

- Bring the water for the pasta to a boil. Put a little oil in a frying pan and cook the sausages for a couple of minutes. Cut them into one-inch pieces and continue frying until a little crispy on the outside and cooked through out. Set aside. Put one tablespoon of oil, the red chillies and the chestnuts in the same pan and cook for about two minutes until cooked through. Salt liberally and set aside. Put another tablespoon of oil in the same pan, the garlic and the beet greens and cook a couple of minutes until they wilt and soften. Combine the sausage and the chestnuts in the pan with the beet greens and a couple more tablespoons of oil and cover to keep warm. Turn off heat. Place the pasta in the water. Stir frequently. Cook until al dente. Drain the pasta and toss in the pan with the sausage, chestnuts and beet greens. Serve on a plate with grated parmesan cheese and parsley to garnish.

Trafilata al bronzo is a spaghetti-length fusilli.

♪nOte: It goes without saying (but I'm saying it anyway) that all the above recipes will work equally well with any kind of pasta. I like experimenting.

Tagliatelle Puttanesque!

INGREDIENTS

400 g tagliatelle
2 tbsp olive oil
2 garlic cloves, chopped
1 small red bird's eye chili (deseeded, if you prefer a more mild heat)
1 tbsp fresh rosemary, finely chopped
8 anchovy fillets, finely chopped
12 black olives, pitted and halved
2 tbsp capers, in salt, rinsed
700 ml tomato passata
grated parmesan

METHOD

- Cook pasta in large pot of salted boiling water until al dente.
- Drain and set aside some of the water.
- Heat oil in pan of medium heat, add garlic and stir, careful not to burn (10 seconds).
- Add rosemary, chili and anchovies. Mash anchovies.
- Add olives and capers. Stir.
- Add passata and simmer a couple of minutes.
- Toss pasta through the sauce, adding some reserved pasta water if necessary to keep it a little loose.

Serve with grated parmesan.

Strascinate di Cascia
(The carbonara)

The classic origin dish for Spaghetti Carbonara from the 15th century. The back-flavours of lemon and nutmeg, combined with the coarse hand-cut pasta, set this apart from the egg & bacon restaurant versions. And the guanciale!

INGREDIENTS
200 g handmade pasta, (200 g flour, 1 egg, some water)
2 tbsp olive oil
50 g guanciale (or pancetta), finely diced
50 g Italian sausage, (fennel is nice), broken into bits (optional)
salt & pepper
1 egg
2 egg yolks
juice of ½ lemon
grated nutmeg
parmesan or pecorino cheese, grated
finely chopped parsley, for garnish

METHOD

- Make the pasta. This is as easy as making a chapati so don't give up yet. Mound the flour on the table, make a well in the centre, break in the egg and a little water and gradually mix to a smooth dough. Add water as needed until it holds together. Roll out into a flat sheet about 1 ½ mm thick. Let rest 20 minutes. Dust both sides. Roll into a cylinder on a chopstick (or something long and thin) and then slice into 3 cm wide strips. (Make sure you take out the chopstick first; it makes it much easier to slice. Boom boom!) Shake out the strands and dust with flour. Hang individual strands outside on a broom handle to dry for 20 minutes while you prepare the rest of the ingredients.

- Bring pot of salted water to boil.

- Mix egg and egg yolks with lemon juice and some nutmeg in a small bowl.

- Heat oil in pan and fry the guanciale. Add the sausage, if using. Fry until browned.

- Cook pasta until *al dente*. Drain and add to the pan of sausage (off the heat), toss and then stir in the eggs and lemon juice. Toss well. Allow to rest a few minutes. Serve with grated parsley.

Pasta broom

Cut pasta

Nuit étoilée

♪nOte: Roll the pasta sheet extra thin and use a star-shaped pastry nozzle as a punch to make this original Dolce-designed pasta, Nuit étoilée, for soups. (What Vincent van Gogh might have come up with if he had been an Italian nonna.)

Grilled Eggplant Slices

This is a quicky for the barbie.

INGREDIENTS

2 eggplants, sliced into quarter-inch rounds
½ cup olive oil
fresh sprigs of rosemary
salt and pepper
2 cloves of garlic, chopped finely

METHOD

- Spread the eggplant slices on newspaper, and salt thoroughly.
- Allow to rest for 20 minutes to draw out the water. Pat dry.
- Heat up an outdoors grill or grill-pan.
- Mix eggplant with olive oil, chopped rosemary, salt, pepper and garlic and allow to marinate for fifteen minutes.
- Grill the eggplant slices and serve with the Yogurt-Garlic sauce.

Eggplant Parmesan

Another of the great Italian comfort foods. The thick eggplant slices browned in a fresh breadcrumb coating, and baked until fork-tender, are like a vegetarian filet mignon. Prepare this one and…. get thyself comfortable!

INGREDIENTS

eggplant, thick slices (½ inch)
flour, for dredging
mixture of fresh and dried bread crumbs
2-3 beaten eggs, as needed
olive oil
salt
grated parmesan cheese
about a litre of tomato passata or puree
chicken bones
oven proof casserole dish, with lid, for baking

METHOD

sauce:

Place chicken bones in tomato passata. (If you want a vegetarian sauce, omit the chicken bones and sauté some diced onions in olive oil first.) Add bay leaf, salt and pepper, fresh basil leaves, a little red or white wine, garlic, or red chili -anything you want to give the sauce a more distinctive flavour. Simmer for about an hour or until the meat drops off the bones. Strain sauce. If you want you can pick the bits of chicken off the bones, dice it, and put the meat back in the sauce.

eggplant:

Place the slices on a flat surface and sprinkle salt over the top. Leave for about 15 minutes. This helps eliminate some bitterness. Wipe dry with paper towels. Three step coating: dip eggplant in flour, then in beaten egg, and finally in breadcrumbs. Fry in hot olive oil until golden brown on both sides. (It is not necessary that they are cooked all the way through as they still have to be baked.) Drain on paper and set aside.

assembly:

Spread some sauce in the bottom of the casserole dish. Then a layer of eggplant, a layer of sauce, and a layer of grated cheese. Repeat this until all the eggplant is used. (The top should have a layer of grated cheese.) Cover.
(The above three steps can be done in advance).
Preheat oven to 200°C. Bake casserole in oven for 45 minutes. Serve hot or cold and tastes even *better* the next day, so make a lot. Use the best ingredients and you will get the best flavours.

Aphrodite's Magic Girdle Moussaka

If you eat too much of this addictive Greek comfort food, with its rich bechamel sauce, you're going to need a magical girdle.

INGREDIENTS

2 medium eggplants
olive oil
2 medium onions, peeled and sliced
500 g beef/pork mince
2 tbsp tomato paste
¾ cup beef stock
250 g potatoes, peeled and cooked, sliced
2 tomatoes, sliced
salt and pepper
1 tsp mixed herbs (dried and fresh oregano, fresh sage and parsley)

bechamel sauce:

30 g butter
30 g plain flour
30 g grated cheese
1 ½ cups milk
2 eggs, separated
⅛ teas mixed herbs (dried oregano, nutmeg, fresh sage)
1 bay leaf

METHOD

- Preheat oven to moderate.
- Slice the eggplant and spread on a plate. Sprinkle with salt and leave for fifteen minutes. Rinse and dry.
- Fry the eggplant in the olive oil until brown on both sides and set aside. Add oil as needed.
- Add a little more oil to the pan, if required, and cook the onion until soft. Add the mince and cook until browned. Stir in the tomato paste, stock, herbs and seasonings.
- Bring to the boil. Cover and simmer for 15 minutes.
- Layer the bottom of an oven-proof casserole with half the eggplant. Pour over half the meat mixture and top with sliced tomatoes.
- Add the remainder of the eggplant and meat, and layer with the sliced potatoes.

bechamel sauce:
- Infuse the milk with a bay leaf, nutmeg, and herbs beforehand.
- Melt the butter, stir in the flour and gradually blend in the milk. Bring the sauce to the boil, stirring constantly. Remove from heat. Beat in the egg yolks and cheese.
- Whisk the egg whites separately and gently fold into the sauce.
- Pour the sauce over the layered eggplant and meat, and bake in a moderate oven for 45 minutes or until golden brown. If the top browns too fast, place a piece of aluminium foil over the top.

Basic thing to remember: all the ingredients are already cooked, more or less. The baking time is primarily to heat and combine flavours and in this instance, to firm up the bechamel custard.

Knife penny

Stir with a knife and stir up strife.
anon

Never close a knife if someone else has opened it.
Two knives crossed on an Irish table cause a quarrel.
Two knives crossed on an Italian table insult the Cross.
A knife crossed with a spoon indicates bad food - curse on the cook.
A knife in a cradle's headboard guards the baby.
Black-handled knives under Grecian pillows keep away nightmares.
Bad luck to say the word knife while at sea.
Bad luck to buy a knife and not first cut wood or paper.
Bad fortune to sharpen a blade in Mississippi after sundown.
Bad omen to scour a butcher's knife.
Good fortune to find a knife, no matter how useless and old - keep it.
A Russian knife lying sharp side up augurs the birth of a murderer.
A knife left lying on its back cuts an angel's foot.
Playing with a Romanian knife causes an angel to flee.
Licking food off a Ukrainian knife makes you cruel and angry like a dog.
Sleeping above a Chinese knife scares away evil spirits.
Presenting a knife to a Japanese colleague suggests suicide.
Navajo knives are used only to cut, never to stab food, or as forks.
Dull knives, in Jamaican kitchens, indicate husband's worthlessness in bed.
Touching oneself with a knife, in Madagascar, causes leprosy.
A knife in a jar of water wards off evil spirits afraid of reflections.
A knife given as a gift severs friendship - unless a coin is taped to the blade.
A combat knife placed back in its sheath before drawing blood will fail you in battle.
A Chinese knife that has slain a person is precious.
You never truly own a knife until it has bitten you.

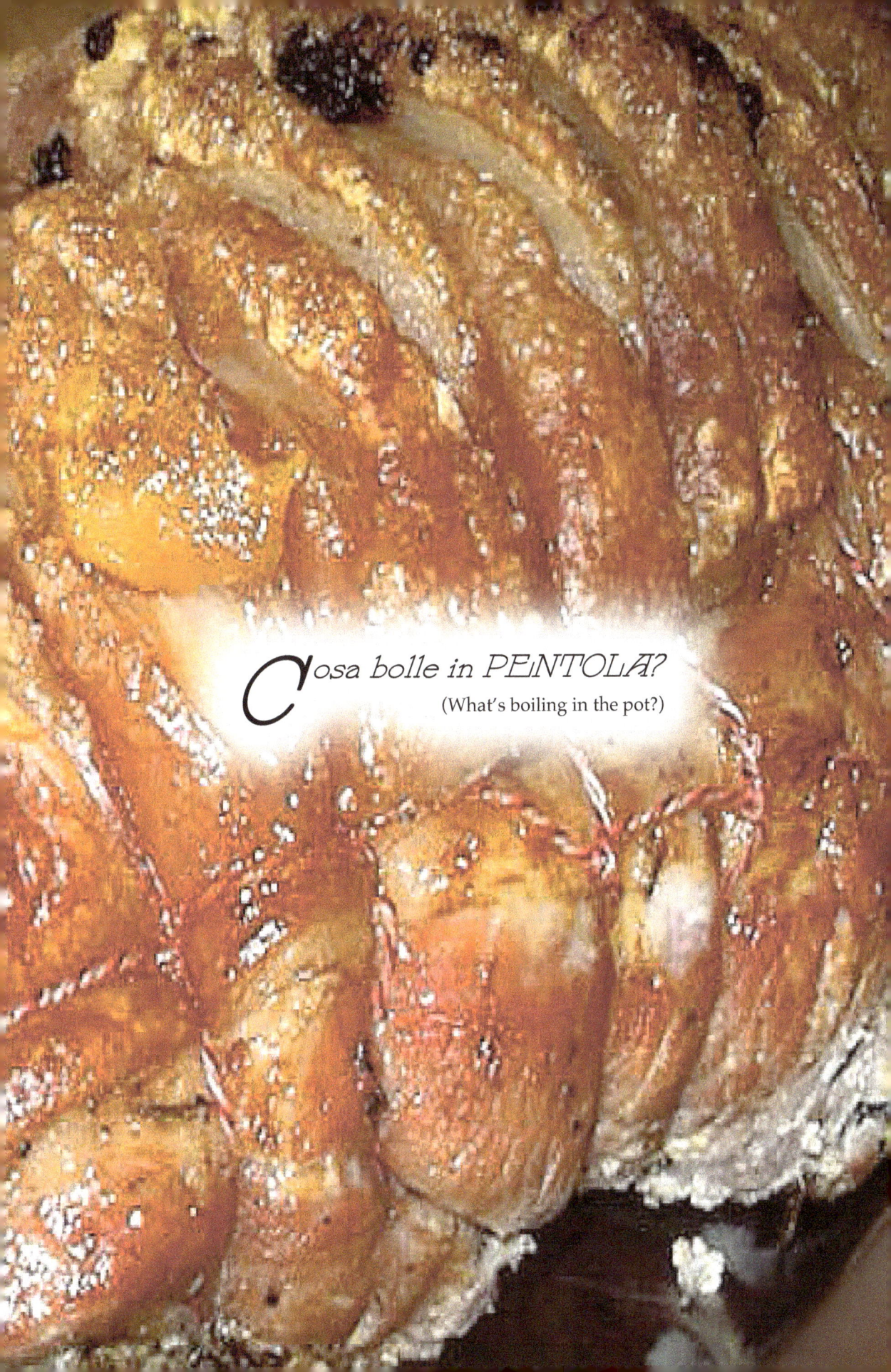

Cosa bolle in PENTOLA?
(What's boiling in the pot?)

New England Corned Beef & Cabbage Boiled Dinner

This is one of the most mouth-watering dishes I know. I've been preparing it since the mid-70s. I first saw it in an old Time-Life magazine and have continually reinvented it over the past fifty years. It was the first time I actually stopped to think that maybe the USA actually had its own distinctive cuisine. (This was of course before I discovered the miracle of Soul Food.) It is also an example of one of those core dishes that I no longer need a recipe for because I have made it for half my life! Served on a large oval-shaped metal tray. It's a great festive dish for family gatherings.

INGREDIENTS
3 ½ pounds corned beef brisket or corned silverside
15 peppercorns
8 whole cloves
bay leaf
parsley, minced
10 baby beets
10 small new potatoes, peeled
10 small carrots, peeled
10 small onions
1 small head cabbage, cut into quarters

METHOD

- Put the brisket in a 5 or 6 quart Dutch oven and cover with an inch of water. Add peppercorns, cloves, and a bay leaf to the pot. Bring to a simmer, cover and lower the heat until barely simmering. Keep at a low simmer for four hours or until the meat is tender (fork-tender).

- Remove the meat and set aside, keeping it warm. Check the broth for taste. If it is too salty, add a little more water to taste. Raise the temperature and bring the broth to a high simmer. Add the potatoes and onions to the pot. Cook for ten minutes. Add the carrots and cabbage and cook for another ten minutes or until all the vegetables are tender. Cook the beets separately in boiling water in their own pan. Squeeze off the skins. Remove the vegetables and keep warm.

Slice the meat in thin slices against the grain. Place sliced meat on a large serving dish surrounded by onions, potatoes, carrots, cabbage quarters and beets. Sprinkle some minced fresh parsley over the top. Serve with horseradish, mustards, garlic dill pickles, sour cream and other condiments of your choice.

Horseradish Sauce

INGREDIENTS
3 tbsp prepared horseradish
¼ cup sour cream
1 tsp Dijon mustard
1 tbsp mayonnaise
1 tbsp chives or scallions, chopped finely
mix together

Lin's Hot Paprika Goulash

This recipe is one of the most memorable comfort foods of our Melbourne family. Lin van Hek was taught this basic recipe from her grandmother and has cooked it for half her life. During that time, it has evolved into her own personal creation, which is a richer, hotter one-pot extravaganza. If you ask her children which dish they remember most fondly from their childhood, it is this one.

The meat is cooked in two parts: the first part to enrich the casserole; the second part to add juicy eye fillet morsels to the final dish.

INGREDIENTS
olive oil
4 brown onions, chopped finely
garlic, chopped roughly
½ inch fresh ginger, sliced
hot paprika
sweet paprika
smoked paprika
3 very hot red chillies, sliced
some flour
300 g stewing steak, cut in small pieces
3 yellow bell peppers (capsicums), cut into chunks
3 red bell peppers (capsicums), cut into chunks
3 green bell peppers (capsicums), cut into chunks
celery, chopped
½ cup dry white wine
some water
3 tomatoes, chopped
potatoes, cut into small pieces
baby carrots, half left whole, half cut into rounds
200 g eye fillet steak, cut in small pieces
3 pale green banana peppers, cut into strips
4 red onions, cut into wedges
sour cream
salt and pepper to taste

METHOD

part 1:

- Heat oil in large casserole.

- Brown onions, garlic, ginger and 3 paprika spices at the same time. Mix while stirring.

- Add one hot chili.

- Toss stewing steak in flour to coat generously. Shake off excess flour. Add meat to casserole. Stir well.

- Add the three coloured bell peppers and celery to pot. Stir until well mixed.

- When meat is thoroughly browned, add wine and some water to just cover. Cover with lid, bring to a simmer and reduce heat to low.

- Cook for 1½ hours.
- Keep an eye on it. Add more water (if necessary).
- After 1½ hours, turn off heat. Let rest.
- Add tomatoes, 2 remaining hot chillies, potatoes and carrot rounds.
- Bring back to simmer and reduce heat to low.
- Cook for another 45 minutes or until potatoes break down.
- Add salt to taste.

part 2:
- Toss eye fillet pieces in flour and shake off excess.
- In a separate pan, fry until brown.
- Add to casserole.
- Add whole baby carrots, banana peppers and red onions.
- Fold in two large tbsp of sour cream. Serve hot in a wide bowl with garnishes.

garnishes:

Fresh parsley, sweet paprika powder and sour cream.

left-over magic:

When we visited Austria, back in the 80s, there was an unforgettable Goulash Soup at our small hotel. With the addition of a little stock or even some water, you can turn this goulash, on the following day, into a warming soup.

Osso Buco Milanese-Style

There are no tomatoes in this dish. Instead of beef shanks, use veal shanks and add a gremolata at the end for extra flavour.

INGREDIENTS
12 pieces veal shank, about 4 cm thick
plain flour, seasoned with salt and pepper
60 ml olive oil (don't skimp!)
60 g butter (don't skimp!)
1 garlic clove
250 ml dry white wine
1 bay leaf
pinch of allspice
pinch of ground cinnamon

gremolata:

2 tsp grated lemon rind
6 tbsp finely chopped parsley
1 garlic glove, finely chopped

To make the gremolata, mix together the lemon rind, parsley and garlic.

METHOD

- Tie each piece of veal shank around the middle with string.
- Dust with seasoned flour.
- Heat oil, butter and garlic in a large saucepan (with a lid) big enough to hold the shanks in one layer.
- Brown the shanks for about 10-15 minutes.
- Arrange shanks standing up in the pan in a single layer.
- Pour in the wine, add the bay leaf, allspice and cinnamon. Cover the pan.
- Cook at a low simmer for 15 minutes.
- Add 125 ml warm water.
- Continue cooking, covered, for 45 minutes to one hour, until the meat is tender. You may want to continue to cook this for an additional hour or so if you really like your meat fork-tender. In that case, every 20 minutes, check level of water and add more if needed.
- Transfer veal to plate and keep warm.
- Discard garlic clove and bay leaf.

- Increase heat under saucepan and stir for a couple of minutes until the sauce is thick, scraping up any bits on the bottom of the pan.
- Stir in the gremolata.
- Check seasoning, adding salt and pepper taste, and return veal to the pan.
- Heat through and serve with lemon wedges.

Irish Lamb Stew

INGREDIENTS

1 ½ pounds thickly sliced bacon, diced
6 pounds boneless lamb shoulder, cut into 2 inch pieces. Use a good cut because, as the Irish proverb says: *Ni dhéanfadh an saol capall rása d'asal* (you cannot make a racehorse out of a donkey).
½ tsp salt
½ tsp ground black pepper
½ cup all-purpose flour
3 cloves garlic, minced
1 large onion, chopped
1 ½ cups water
4 cups beef stock
2 tsp white sugar
4 cups diced carrots
2 large onions, cut into bite-size pieces
3 potatoes
1 tsp dried thyme
2 bay leaves
1 cup white wine

METHOD

- Place bacon in a large, deep skillet. Cook over medium high heat until evenly brown. Drain, crumble, and set aside.
- Put lamb, salt, pepper, and flour in large mixing bowl.
- Toss to coat meat evenly.
- Brown meat in frying pan with bacon fat. Place meat into stock pot (leave ¼ cup of fat in frying pan).
- Add the garlic and yellow onion and sauté till onion begins to become golden.
- Deglaze frying pan with ½ cup water and add the garlic-onion mixture to the stock pot with bacon pieces, beef stock, and sugar.
- Cover and simmer for 1 ½ hours. Add carrots, onions, potatoes, thyme, bay leaves, and wine to pot.
- Reduce heat and simmer covered for 20 minutes until vegetables are tender.

Lamb Shanks w/ Mashed Potatoes

INGREDIENTS
2 lamb shanks, in one piece
cooking string
olive oil
1 red onion, sliced
handful of raisins
1 tbsp marmalade
1 tbsp tomato sauce (ketchup)
1 tbsp Worcestershire sauce
70 ml beer or stout
650 ml chicken stock
fresh rosemary sprig
salt and pepper
fresh mint leaves

METHOD

- Tie shanks with string so they don't fall apart. Brown in a pot in olive oil.
- Remove shanks from pot.
- Sauté red onion in same pan until soft and caramelised.
- Add a little extra oil if required. Add raisins & marmalade. Add tomato sauce/ketchup. Add Worcestershire sauce. Add beer/stout.
- Season with salt, pepper & a fresh rosemary sprig. Add shanks back to pot. Add chicken stock. Cover & simmer over lower heat.
- Cook 3 hours (turn shanks halfway).
- Half hour before ready, boil some potatoes for mash. Remove shanks.
- Whiz up sauce, reduce heat & thicken. (If sauce is too thin, either keep cooking until reduced, or pour half out or thicken with some corn starch mixed in a little cold water.
- Put shanks back in to reheat. Mash potatoes.

mint oil:

- Place fresh mint into mortar & pestle. Bash up. Add 3-5 tbsp olive oil.
- Serve shanks (with string removed) upright on mashed potatoes.
- Drizzle over sauce.
- Drizzle over mint oil.

Ethiopian Leg of Lamb
w/ Berbere Spices & Mint Sauce

Someone once said that if Colonel Sanders had been African, he would have used the twelve spices in the Berbere spice mix.

INGREDIENTS
leg of lamb
½ cup Berbere spice
olive oil
fresh rosemary
4 cloves garlic
lemon
salt

Berbere spice mix:

1 tsp ground cardamon
1 tsp coriander seeds
1 tsp cumin seeds
1 tsp fenugreek seeds
½ tsp ajowan seeds (optional)
10 small dried chillies
1 tsp allspice
½ tsp ground nutmeg
1 tsp ginger
2 tsp black peppercorns
8 cloves
2 tbsp sea salt

METHOD

- Toast the whole spices in a heavy-based frying pan over a medium heat until they just begin to change colour and give off a rich aroma. Grind to a fine powder in a mortar and pestle. Roughly cut up the dried chillies, discard some of the seeds, pound them in the mortar and pestle, then mix together with the remaining ingredients.

- Preheat the oven to 220°C.

- Cut the garlic into long wedges. With a small knife, make inserts in the lamb and poke in a garlic wedge. Rub the leg of lamb with the berbere spices on all sides. Place in a roasting pan.

- Put a good splash of olive oil over it and roll in the pan until well-coated. (Roll the lamb in the pan as well, boom boom!)

- Roast for around an hour, turning every twenty minutes or so - (tip: turn the roast as well, boom boom!) - or until the juices run slightly clear when the meat is pierced with a knife. Take out of the oven and rest before carving. Serve with **Yogurt-Garlic** sauce on the side, roast potatoes & pumpkin with rosemary, mint sauce and a green salad.

Mint Sauce

INGREDIENTS

6 tbsp sugar
6 tbsp water
handful fresh mint leaves, chopped finely
few slice of red chili
1 tbsp vinegar

METHOD

- Bring water and sugar to boil. Lower to simmer and stir. When bubbles cover the surface of the pan, add vinegar and reduce to taste. Remove from heat and add mint and chillies. If too thin, for your taste, reduce over heat for a little longer. Cool.

Eric's Steak
w/ Peppercorns & Cream

I learned this wonderful way to prepare eye fillet from one of our extended family relatives, Eric van Hecke, from Belgium.

INGREDIENTS
2 eye fillet steaks
butter
1-2 tablespoons green (or red) peppercorns for each steak
½ cup fresh cream
1 egg yolk

METHOD

- Melt 2 tbsp of butter in a skillet, add the green peppercorns and the steaks and cook the way you like them.
- Remove meat from pan and cover with foil.
- Reduce heat. Add the cream, scraping the bits from the bottom.
- Add the beaten egg yolk.
- Heat for a minute or two until the sauce reduces a little.
- Pour sauce over the steaks.

Serve with mashed potatoes.

Breaded Veal Schnitzels

This was one of my mother's memorable comfort food dishes. There would always be a heaping plate of these schnitzels (or 'cutlets', as Italians call them) in the refrigerator to eat cold with bread and hot peppers, whenever I visited home.

INGREDIENTS

tender veal schnitzels
milk
flour
eggs
freshly made bread-crumbs, from fresh bread
fresh parsley, chopped finely
salt and pepper
sweet paprika
olive oil, for frying

METHOD

- Place each slice of veal between two pieces of plastic wrap and pound flat, but not too thin.
- Put the flour on one flat plate and season with salt and pepper.
- Put the eggs in a shallow bowl and beat well. (Add some milk if you like.)
- Place the breadcrumbs in another shallow bowl and season with parsley and paprika.
- Dreg the veal in flour, shake off extra; then dip in the egg and then in the breadcrumbs, patting the breadcrumbs down lightly.
- Place in the refrigerator until ready to fry.
- Heat oil in large frypan.
- Fry veal on both sides until golden.
- Drain on paper towels.

In Estonia, they serve these with lightly-tossed steamed potatoes and a Russian dressing.

Russian Dressing:

INGREDIENTS
½ cup mayonnaise
3 tbsp tomato sauce (ketchup)
2 tbsp horseradish
2 tsp Worcestershire sauce
1 tbsp sugar
¼ tsp sweet paprika
sea salt & black pepper

METHOD
- Whisk together mayonnaise, ketchup, horseradish, Worcestershire, sugar and paprika until combined.
- Season with salt and pepper.

Veal Muscat Dolce
w/ Mushrooms, Shallots, Red Chili, Kaffir Lime Leaf, Mashed Sweet Potatoes & Green Beans

This makes a nice variation to the more traditional Veal Marsala. The sweetness of the muscat gravy, with just hint of kaffir lime leaf, is echoed wonderfully in the sweet potatoes and the ginger, contrasted with the crunchiness of the beans and almonds. The veal against the bright oranges and greens of the sweet potato and beans also make a colourful presentation.

Prep your ingredients and timings well as you want all three dishes to finish approx. the same time.

INGREDIENTS
thinly pounded veal slices, cut in small pieces
flour, for dredging
muscat wine
button mushrooms, both sliced and whole
2 tbsp butter
olive oil
shallots, finely sliced
½ red chili, finely chopped
1 kaffir lime leaf, very finely slivered
salt & pepper
½ lime
fresh coriander, finely chopped, for garnish

METHOD
- Dredge veal slices in flour. Shake off excess.
- Brown the mushrooms in a little butter and keep warm.
- Heat the olive oil in a clean pan until smoking.
- Fry the shallots and the red chili until the shallots are almost crisp.
- Remove to absorbent paper. In the same pan, brown veal on both sides, until cooked through. Remove veal and set aside. Scrap bits from the pan.
- Add as much muscat as you want (between half cup to a cup or more), some salt and pepper and the kaffir lime leaf.
- Stir well and return the veal, mushrooms and the shallots to the pan and simmer until the sauce is reduced and slightly thickened into a nice gravy. (Add more muscat if necessary and further reduce). Check seasoning.

Sweet Potatoes w/Ginger:

INGREDIENTS

3 sweet potatoes
butter
piece of finely chopped fresh ginger
salt & freshly ground pepper

METHOD

≡ Peel the potatoes, cut into small pieces and boil until soft. Drain, add some butter, salt and pepper, the ginger and mash roughly. Keep warm.

Green Beans w/Almonds:

INGREDIENTS

fresh green beans
½ cup sliced almonds
butter
salt and freshly ground pepper

METHOD

≡ Pinch off the stems of the beans and wash well. Steam in a little water with the pot covered. Do not overcook - keep them crisp. Remove from the heat, drain the water and refresh in some cold water. Drain and add the butter, the almonds and the salt and pepper. Keep warm with a tea towel but do not cover as you want them crisp, not overcooked in their own steam.

BBQ Spareribs
w/ Red-Eye Gravy

Back in the 80s, I visited Harlem, New York, and had lunch at Sylvia's Soul Food Restaurant. The taxi driver who drove me there from my hotel in Greenwich Village asked me why a white boy would want to go that far into Harlem. His actual words were, 'are you tired of looking pretty?' I had rung ahead and made a booking and was told that someone would meet me in front of the restaurant. The taxi dropped me off at the address I had and drove away in a hurry but when I looked up, I was standing in front of a boarded-up building. Across the street, there was a gang of eight tough looking teens, wearing red bandanas on their heads, sitting on the steps in front of a tenement building, watching me. Just when I was getting that feeling of impending 'unprettiness', the big impeccably-dressed black maître d' of Sylvia's came around the corner and guided me to the correct entrance. They had been expecting me.

I think I ordered a 'tasting' menu of forty dishes spread over two tables. It cost about $300 in 1980s money. The place was packed with elegantly attired older couples. I was the only white person there. They must have thought I was crazy. One friendly grandmotherly-like lady said, 'Son, you sure must be hungry.' But there was a method to the madness: I wanted to taste how these classic Southern soul food dishes were supposed to be made, by someone who knew what they were doing.

Later, following easily available recipes, in books and online, and now with this 'sense-memory', I was able to recreate them myself.

bbq sauce (4-5 cups):

INGREDIENTS
450 ml of any good hot sauce (like Franks or Louisiana Hot Sauce)
3 cups thin unseasoned tomato puree
1 ½ cups water
1 ½ cups sugar
1 sliced lemon
1 stalk celery
1 onion
2 ½ teas red pepper flakes

METHOD
- Mix all ingredients in a good-sized pot. Heat until just before boiling but don't boil or else the sauce will darken. Cool. Strain. Put in a bottle with a lid in the fridge.

ribs:

INGREDIENTS

3 ½ lbs (2 slabs) American pork spareribs, have the butcher cut them down the middle of the slab, to make them easier to handle.
2-3 cups white vinegar, to cover
½ teas red pepper flakes
½ teas ground black pepper
1 ½ teas salt

night before:

METHOD

- Rub salt, black pepper and red pepper flakes into both sides of ribs, cover and refrigerate overnight.

- Preheat oven to hottest. (250°C). Place ribs in large, flat baking pan. Pour vinegar over the ribs and bake for about an hour. Turn them a couple of times and spoon pan juices over the top. (This step gives the ribs a vinegary flavour.)

- Remove ribs from pan and place in a single layer on baking sheets, lined with aluminium foil. Bake at 250°C for one hour or less. Watch them. Ribs should be well-browned but not burnt. (These 2 steps can be done in advance.)

finish:

- Lower the heat to 200°C.
- Cut the slabs, between the bones, into individual ribs.
- Place the ribs in a large baking dish to fit in a single layer if possible.
- Spoon enough bbq sauce over them to coat lightly.
- Cover the pan with foil and bake until heated through, about 20 minutes.

♪nOte: once you have baked the ribs in this sauce, it will have an incredibly rich flavour which can be kept in the fridge and used on many other dishes, such as ham steak, fried eggs or potato salad.

variation: Use the above recipe but embellish it with a Red-eye Gravy BBQ Sauce.

Red-eye Gravy BBQ Sauce Accelerator

METHOD

- Reduce a couple slices of bacon, guanciale or pancetta, in a pan, and remove the meat.
- Add ½ cup coffee and stir for a minute.
- Add it to the bbq sauce above, before the final bake, and stir to mix.

Brown Sugar, Maple Syrup & Cinnamon Glazed Ham

INGREDIENTS

1 x 7 ½ kg ham
14 cloves
200 ml pure Maple syrup
3 tbsp seeded mustard
1 tbsp cinnamon
200 ml pineapple juice
200 g brown sugar
1 fresh, ripe pineapple, sliced, or one small can of pineapple slices

For those of you who get confused about ham and smoked ham, they are the same thing. All ham is smoked, precooked and ready to eat. All we are doing here is glazing an already cooked ham. An idiot-proof recipe. This can be prepared the night before and cooked four hours before the meal. One of the easiest and most show-stopping dishes I know.

A decent ham should have about 2 cm of fat on top (under the skin).

METHOD

- Remove the skin.
- Criss-cross score it or make 14 crosses into the fat and insert the cloves at the intersections. In a bowl, mix the maple syrup, mustard, cinnamon and pineapple juice. Brush the mixture evenly over the ham using a pastry brush. Place in the fridge and leave for 12 hours or overnight. When ready to cook the ham, preheat the oven to 180°C. Remove the meat from the fridge and spread the brown sugar evenly on top. Bake for an hour and fifteen minutes. Rest for 3 hours before serving.
- Remove the meat from the fridge, spread the brown sugar evenly on top and affix the pineapple slices to the ham with toothpicks. Bake for an hour and fifteen minutes, basting every 20 minutes. Rest for 3 hours before serving.

Roast Pork w/Crackle & Gravy

INGREDIENTS
1 medium pork roast (with skin, scored)
olive oil
salt and pepper
water or chicken stock
dried chili flakes
potatoes, cut in half, and parboiled slightly, for roasting
onions, cut in half, for roasting
carrots, for roasting
pumpkin, cut in wedges, for roasting
1 onion, diced finely for gravy

Place vegetables in separate roasting pan, drizzle olive oil over top and season with salt and pepper

how to get a perfect crackle: METHOD

- Score fat deeply, almost down to the meat. Salt the pork well and place in fridge overnight. In the morning, wipe it dry.
- Preheat the oven to hottest temperature. Place the roast skin-side up on a wire rack in the sink and pour boiling water over it.
- Wipe dry. Place pork in roasting pan and massage some olive oil, salt & pepper all over the meat and let rest for 30 minutes. Place pan in oven and cook for 50 minutes. Place vegetables in oven, in a separate pan, at the same time and do preliminary roasting for 30 minutes.
- Remove vegetables from oven. Remove the roast from the oven, pour off some of the fat, to use for the gravy and return roast to oven. Turn heat down to 180°C. Check crackle. (If done, remove it and return roast to oven.) Roast for 50 minutes more at lower heat or until done the way you like it.
- Pan-fry the potatoes in a little oil and return to vegetable tray. Thirty minutes before the roast is ready, return the vegetables to the oven to finish.
- Make the gravy by putting some fat into a separate pan, heating it up and adding 2-3 tbsp of flour. Stir to make a roux and add water or stock, chili flakes, salt and pepper. Stir well until the gravy is at the thickness you like.
- Remove meat to a cutting board, remove crackle and place in a separate dish. Cover meat and let rest. Place vegetables in a serving dish and keep warm. Place gravy in a heated serving bowl, slice the roast and serve with vegetables and a side of applesauce.

Smothered Pork Chops

INGREDIENTS
8 ¾ inch shoulder pork chops
1 tsp, plus 1 tbsp salt
1 tsp, plus 1 tbsp freshly ground black pepper
2 cups, plus 2 tablespoons plain flour
½ cup olive oil
2 large onions, coarsely chopped
2 green bell peppers, cored, seeded and coarsely chopped
2 stalks celery, coarsely chopped
2 green chiles
2 jalapeño peppers, seeded and coarsely chopped
2 cups water
½ tsp red chilli flakes (optional)

METHOD

- Trim the excess fat from the edges of the pork chops. Season them with salt and pepper. Season 2 cups of the flour with salt and pepper.

- Dredge the pork chops in the flour until coated on all sides.

- Shake off excess four. Pour the oil into a heavy skillet (cast-iron is good) over medium high heat. When the oil begins to shake slightly, add as many pork chops as will fit in the pan without touching. Fry, turning once, until well browned on both sides, about 5 minutes.

- Remove the chops to a plate and repeat with the remaining chops. Pour off all but 4 tbsp of fat from the skillet.

- Reduce the heat to medium and add the onions, green peppers, green chiles, celery and optional red chilli flakes to the skillet.

- Cook until brown and tender, about 10 minutes.

- Move the vegetables to one side of the skillet and sprinkle 2 tbsp of flour over the bottom of the skillet.

- Add another tbsp or two of oil, if necessary. Cook the flour until golden brown, stirring constantly and being careful not to let the flour burn. Slowly pour in the water and stir until you have a smooth gravy. Divide the pork chops between two heavy skillets with lids or place them all in a large heavy Dutch oven.

- Top with the gravy and vegetables and cover tightly. Simmer over low heat until the vegetables are tender and the pork chops are cooked through, about 15 minutes. Check the seasoning and add salt and pepper as necessary. Serve spooning some of the gravy and vegetables over each chop.

Pig tails in gravy

Pig tails in gravy
ain't that hard to cook,
remember this song
and you won't need no recipe book.

Two pounds of tails for a pig tail treat,
cut each pig tail into three or four piece.
One large onion, a stalk of celery,
chop it coarsely, as coarse as can be.

Four cups water, quarter cup of vinegar,
add the onions, celery, pig tails and stir.
Black pepper, salt, a teaspoon of chili flakes,
cover and simmer - takes an hour to make.

Preheat your oven, take the tails from the broth,
bake 'em at 350, until the fat browns off.
A third cup of flour, a third of water too,
mix to a paste and stir until smooth.

Stir up your flour paste into your broth,
stir it until your gravy gets smooth and soft.
Add the tails to the gravy, simmer on low heat,
in fifteen minutes, check your seasoning and eat.

Pig tails in gravy
ain't that hard to cook,
remember this song
and you won't need no recipe book.

♩=120

animato

Pigtails

C ... **F**

CHORUS: Pigtails in gravy ain't that hard to

(VOCAL) ♩. **G**

...quieter Bass...

you   won't need

C

VERSE: Two pounds of tails for a

G

cut each pigtail into

Gravy

Ragout des Pattes de Porc

For those of you who aren't musically declined, here's a simple variation of pigs' feet, with an elegant name, and an even stranger story, that I recall from the *1965 Catholic Cookbook* when I attended St Mary's in Painesville, Ohio. It is a tribute to 'Tantony', the nickname of St. Anthony the Abbot, one of the Egyptian Desert Fathers, in 3 AD, who kept a pig as a close pet to help him remember to say his prayers. Tantony is known as the patron saint of swineherds.

INGREDIENTS
3 pigs' feet, cleaned
2 onions
24 cloves
2 tbsp flour, browned in a little oil

METHOD

- Stud each onion with a dozen cloves.
- Place pigs' feet and onions in large pot and cover with water.
- Cook 2 hours.
- Mix 2 tbsp of the browned flour with 1 cup stock from the pot and add back to the pot.
- Cook 5 minutes, stirring.

Don't forget to say your prayers!

Sausages & Jalapeños

'Damn the jalapeños, full speed ahead.'

INGREDIENTS
A dozen good quality Italian sausages, preferably made with fennel.
A dozen fresh green jalapeño peppers, seeded and sliced
long-ways into strips.

♪nOte: fresh jalapeños can be substituted in just about all recipes
for green capsicum or green bell peppers.

METHOD
≡ Fry the sausages in a pan on the stovetop until almost ready. Toss in the jalapeños and continue until sausages are done to your liking.

The jalapeños can be finished with a slight crunch or soft depending on your taste. They can also be fried unseeded if you like them extra hot.
Excellent for sandwiches.

People who count their CHICKENS before they are hatched act very wisely because chickens run about so absurdly that it is impossible to count them accurately.

Oscar Wilde

The rime of the ancient gooney bird

The land of water, and of fearful hunger, where no swimming creature was to be hooked or crooked.

The fish were here, the fish were there,
The fish were all about:
Our hunger growled, and churned and howled,
But fish we had caught nought!

A great sea-fowl, called the Gooney Bird, comes through the fog, lured by the sailors.

At length I saw a Gooney Bird,   5
Fly o'er the foggy rip,
As though it were a Columbidae,
We lured it with a chip.

The Gooney Bird returneth regularly for a daily snack.

A good South Wind rung up like rhyme;   9
The Gooney Bird did dance,
And every day, for potato cakes,
Came down as in a trance!

The Gooney Bird chokes on a cast off rollie, mistaken for a morsel.

One day it swallowed a fag-butt whole,   13
Lodged sideways in its throat,
The bird spun round delirious
And fell dead on the boat.

The hungry crew endeavour to prepare the stubborn fowl for tea.

We plucked all day and boiled all night,   17
Tight-lipped without a word.
'God save my Aunties Marinade!'
The fowl was tough as curd.

The sailors reluctantly, eat the foul fowl, using available shipboard condiments, and thus, are saved.

Its thigh was stubborn as a boot,   21
The flavour quite absurd,
But with a side of chips and sauce,
We ate that GOONEY BIRD.

Salt Sarcophagus Chicken

Use rock salt not fine salt. Rock salt stays on the outside and forms a shell (whereas coarse regular salt gets into the chicken cavities too much.)

INGREDIENTS
1 medium free-range chicken
rock salt to completely cover (a lot)
1-2 eggs
a couple of handfuls of fennel seeds
3 bunches of fresh herbs (basil, parsley, coriander)
olive oil
2 lemons
fresh garlic

METHOD

- Pre-heat oven to 200°C.
- With a mortar and pestle, pound the fennel seeds. Add to the rock salt in a large bowl. Add one or two beaten eggs and stir thoroughly.
- Pound the herbs and garlic in the mortar. Add the garlic, the juice of one lemon and a little olive oil and pound some more. Totally cover the chicken with the mixture, rubbing it into every cavity. Cut one lemon in half and place it inside the chicken.
- In a large baking pan, spread a quarter inch layer of the rock salt mixture as a base. Rest the chicken on top. Make sure the herbs are covering as much of the chicken surface as possible. Start spooning the rock salt mixture gently over the chicken, packing it down until the chicken is completely encased in a rock salt sarcophagus.
- Place the chicken in the 200°C oven, on the middle tray, and bake for two hours. When it's done, the rock salt will have hardened and the chicken will be cooked perfectly moist with a wonderful infusion of the herbs, fennel, and lemon. Crack the sarcophagus at the table, with a hammer or meat pounder for maximum dramatic effect.

La Mama's Lost Lebanese BBQ Chicken w/Lemon & Garlic

There was a Lebanese take-away and Belly Dance centre across from La Mama Theatre, in Carlton, back in the early 80s, that served this dish in a paper bag. I have never gotten over the incredible flavour bomb of this particular way of barbecuing chicken. I've been looking for the method to recreate it for forty years and I've finally gotten close. I have added some chili flakes and feta as a variation.

INGREDIENTS
1 whole chicken, cut into pieces
¼ cup olive oil
2 tbsp finely chopped fresh garlic
2 tbsp grated lemon zest
pinch crushed red pepper flakes
sea salt and freshly ground black pepper

Finish:

1 tbsp finely chopped fresh garlic
1 tbsp finely chopped fresh parsley
1 tbsp grated lemon zest
sea salt
medium piece of Persian feta
juice of 1 lemon

METHOD

- Mix together the oil, 1 tbsp of the garlic and 1 tbsp of the lemon zest. Add the chicken and turn to coat in the oil mixture. Cover and let marinate in the refrigerator overnight.

- Next day, about an hour before serving, preheat oven to medium. Oil the bottom of an oven pan and place the chicken pieces evenly spaced. Drizzle a little olive oil over the top and some salt and pepper. Cover with foil and bake for twenty minutes, until the meat is just cooked but still moist.

- Preheat a grill-pan or bbq to hot. Drizzle a little olive oil in the grill-pan. Remove the chicken from the oven pan and reserve pan juices in a large warmed dish. Season both sides of the chicken with salt and pepper. Place the chicken on the grill, skin side down and slowly BBQ, basting with juices, until the fat renders and the skin becomes golden brown and slightly crisp, about 15 minutes. Remove from the grill-pan, cover with foil and let rest 10 minutes.

- To finish, place the chicken pieces in the dish with pan juices. Mix together the remaining garlic and lemon zest and sprinkle over the chicken pieces.
- Remove chicken pieces from the pan and place on a serving dish. Ladle some of the pan juices over the top. Pour the lemon juice over and season to taste with more salt and pepper.
- To serve, scatter the feta pieces around the outside of the chicken and sprinkle with chopped parsley.

Ode to a baccalà
after Dylan Thomas (way after!)

The fat that through the green frog fries the fish,
simmers my salt cod;
no salmon-stream sucking swim up,
but to sleep, to whit, to dream
beneath a salt-sea sand
and I am dumb to tell the dumb dumbwaiter
that at my tablecloth goes
the same crooked carp.

O Baccalà swimming
a dreamfed Dead Sea swamp,
mouth of salt, fish-knifed and filleted
free of gnostic scale,
gutted like a fishy infidel
caught red-finned with mermaid porn,
fish-buried in a barrel's belly,
no Ahab needle to bug-pin and winnow
the Great White Minnow
but to lay four score and seven league
asunder a salty sarcophogas to slumber.

Three apple-dappled days
o' fresh winter's weather water
and it doth suffer a salt-change,
into something chewy and strange,
of its bones is choking made
and I alone live to suck the tail.

Call me Ishmael.
Roll me in cornmael.

Allahhhhh . . .
Baccallahhhhhhhh . . .

Forsooth!
(or for Dante!)
Al dente!
To the tooth!

The first taste is always with the eyes.

Apicius

Baccalà Vesuvio

My rule of thumb for Italian cookbooks: check the contents page to see if there are any baccalà recipes. If not, close the book.

There are three in this book so, rest assured, you are getting the real thing and not a cheap faux-Italian knock off! Satisfaction guaranteed or your pastafazool back.

I hated this dish as a kid even though all the old people in my family loved it. Now I'm an old person, I also love it. Maybe you have to be a bit dried out to appreciate what the poor cod had to go through.

Salted cod. The only fish available in land-locked areas not near the shore until advances such as trucking and freezing. The fish of the poor until relatively recently, converted into the fish of the fairly well-to-do as the traditional dishes gained in prestige and fish stocks started to diminish. Enjoy it while you can because it is gradually become an expensive gourmet dish.

First some baccalà theory.

How salty should the cod be after it's soaked, before you cook it? It's a matter of personal taste.

I buy salt cod from different places and each one has differing amounts of salt saturating the fish. The fish from the gourmet Italian deli around the corner is lightly salted and twenty-four hours of soaking is enough. The big supermarket Safeway baccalà needs about three-four days of soaking as the salt is more deeply embedded. The decision on how long to soak comes from familiarity with what you get from the particular supplier and is trial and error. Three days is probably safe, as a general rule.

If you try to eat salty baccalà after one day of soaking, it will still taste great but you will be chronically thirsty and end up drinking water all day long. When you do soak the fish, you have to change the water 3-4 times a day to get the excess salt out.

Baccalà is different than stockafissio which is the fish you see hanging on hooks that looks like an old cricket bat. Stockafissio is so hard that you can pound nails with it and you have to cut it with a saw. It takes a week to soften. We're talking extra-chewy here, folks! This is a gourmet experience, too.

But the baccalà I use doesn't have this kind of rigor mortis. Salt cod was originally salted to preserve it for lean times and I remember the big barrels filled with baccalà in the neighbourhood grocery shop in Painesville, Ohio, when I was a kid. Obviously, if fish had been plentiful all the time, no one would have ever salted fish in the first place. Fresh cod doesn't have the al dente chewy texture that salted cod has, which is part of the special personality of dried baccalà!

INGREDIENTS

500 g baccalà fillets, soaked with skin removed

1 potato, parboiled, cut into bite-sized chunks

handful black olives, pitted

1 tbsp baby salted capers, rinsed

3 tbsp flour

olive oil

1 onion, chopped finely

1 clove garlic, chopped

3 anchovy fillets

2 bay leaves

fresh basil leaves

1 heaped tsp red chili flakes!

500 ml dry white wine

black pepper

1 can peeled tomatoes

METHOD

- Soak baccalà for three days in water, changing the water a couple of times a day.
- Wipe dry with paper towels and dust in flour.
- Brown in a frying pan in half cup of olive oil.
- Transfer fish to baking dish.
- Mash the anchovies in the frypan oil until they dissolve, add onion and garlic and fry for a couple of minutes. (Don't burn the garlic!)
- Add tomatoes, bay leaf, basil, pepper, capers, olives, chili flakes and simmer 5 minutes.
- Add wine and simmer 5-10 minutes until alcohol evaporates and sauce slightly thickens.
- Add potatoes and pour tomato mix over the top.
- Add more water if necessary.
- Bake uncovered for 20 minutes. Serve with good bread and even better white wine (than the one you cooked with!)

Baccalà, Flamed Tiger Prawns & Fennel Aglio e Olio w/ Spaghettini

The fat, juicy tiger prawns are to kill for and the fennel gives the dish its uniqueness. If you use the salted cod fillets, you must soak them for a day or two. If you use the hard-like-a board stockafissio, I suggest soaking it for a week.

> ♪nOte: the amount of time you soak the fish is personal - if you want a stronger flavour and a little tougher texture, don't soak it as long. The longer you soak, the less salt in the fish.

(This dish can also be made with fresh Ling.)

- Prepare the baccalà in advance. Four salt cod fillets, skin on, soaked for 2-3 days, changing the water a couple times each day. Remove the fish and discard the liquid. Remove any bones. Cut each piece of fish into 1-inch squares so it will be easier to combine with the pasta.

INGREDIENTS
½ cup flour
2 red onions, cut in wedges
3 cloves garlic, halved
3 tomatoes, cut in wedges
½ fennel bulb, finely sliced
¼ cup black and green olives
100 ml white wine
a few strands of saffron, a little turmeric, or, as a last resort, a few drops of yellow food colour
½ cup olive oil
fresh parsley, chopped finely

METHOD

- Rinse fish and pat dry. Preheat oven to 200°C. Coat fish with flour. Heat olive oil in a pan and fry fish for a minute, or so, on each side. Remove fish from pan and keep warm.

- Add remaining ingredients to the pan and sauté a few minutes. Place onions, garlic, tomatoes, fennel, olives and wine mixture in baking dish. Top with the fish, sprinkle with olive oil and parsley. Cover and bake for 15-20 minutes.

to finish:

INGREDIENTS

24 tiger prawns, cleaned and deveined
olive oil
red chili flakes
fennel greens
fettuccini
1 clove of garlic, chopped
chopped parsley

METHOD

- Cook the pasta al dente in a separate pot of boiling water. When the pasta is almost ready, heat olive oil until smoking. Add tiger prawns and toss until the oil catches fire and the prawns are braised in the flames. Add the garlic and toss.

- From the previously prepared pot of baccalà, choose a dozen squares of fish, some tomatoes, some fennel, some olives and spoon some of the sauce into the pan. Add salt and freshly ground black pepper liberally. Toss well. Sprinkle with a liberal dose of olive oil.

- Add the drained pasta to the pan and combine thoroughly.

- Serve with the chopped parsley and fennel greens as garnish.

Chiles en Nogada

For two centuries, this has been the national patriotic dish of Mexico. It was invented in 1821, to celebrate Mexico's independence from Spain. Convent nuns are said to have prepared it for the leader of the Mexican army, Agustín de Iturbide, who later became Mexico's first emperor, Agustín I.

The dish contains the three colors of the Mexican flag: the green of the poblano and parsley, the white of the nogada sauce and the red of the pomegranate seeds.

Prepare the Mexican crema two days in advance.

Mexican Crema:

This is essentially crème fraîche, mixed with lime and salt.

METHOD

≡ Stir together heavy cream and a little yogurt. Then cover the bowl and let it sit at room temperature for two days until it thickens! (It won't spoil since there is acid in the yogurt.) Room temperature is important – if it's too cold, it won't thicken properly. Once it has thickened, stir in the lime juice and salt. It should keep in the fridge for a couple of weeks

for the filling:

INGREDIENTS

283 g beef
283 g pork
1 carrot
1 onion
1 potato
1 zucchini
3 plum tomatoes
½ cup peas
226 g dried fruit
½ cup raisins
½ cup almonds
½ teas cinnamon
1 tbsp brown sugar
6 large poblano chiles
salt

for the nogada sauce:

INGREDIENTS

1 ¼ cup Mexican crema (recipe below)
½ cup walnuts
½ cup cinnamon
1 tbsp brown sugar

for the garnish:

1 large pomegranate
fresh parsley, chopped

METHOD

- Place meat in pan and cover with water.
- Simmer for 20 minutes turning once.
- Remove from pan, cool and reserve meat water.
- Chop meat finely.
- Chop onion, carrot, zucchini, potato and dried fruit into small cubes.
- Chop almonds finely.
- Slice tomatoes and add to blender with ½ cup liquid from meat.
- Blend until smooth.
- Fry the onions in 3 tbsp oil for a few minutes.
- Add the potatoes and cook for 5 minutes.
- Add the chopped meat and mix well.
- Add the pureed tomato.
- Add the carrots, zucchini and raisins and cook five minutes.
- Add the peas and almonds and mix well. Cook 15 minutes.
- If it becomes too dry, add a little more of the liquid from the meat.
- Place chiles over open flame on stove and blacken them.
- Put in a plastic bag to sweat for five minutes.
- Scrape the skin off gently with a knife, keeping the chiles intact.
- Split them down side, from the tip, without cutting through, to make a pocket.
- Remove the seeds and membranes with your fingers without tearing the chiles.

- Place the crema, walnuts and cinnamon in the blender and purée until walnuts and sauce are smooth.
- Break the pomegranates open and remove the bright red seeds. Discard the skin and membranes.
- Chop the parsley very fine.
- Fill each poblano with enough filling so it will just close. Use toothpicks to hold together.
- Place one stuffed chile on each serving plate.
- Spoon nogada sauce over to cover the chile.
- Sprinkle pomegranate seeds and chopped parsley over the top.

Satan's Claws Christmas Baccalà w/Red Jalapeño Peppers & Green Sicilian Olives

I found some red jalapeños peppers and thought of Christmas! Use bright green homemade Sicilian olives which are unpitted and crunchy. The brighter the green, the better.

I warn you. This dish is so aggressive that it will at first offend your palate with an assault of hotness - but you will fatally return to the pot over and over again as your taste buds become accustomed to the abuse and you are seduced by its intensity.

INGREDIENTS
1-2 fillets of baccalà, skin on, (soaked in three changes of water daily over three days, to remove salt.)
20 Sicilian green olives
½ cup of sliced red jalapeño peppers (you can substitute large red chilies (not hot) and a quarter teaspoon of red chili flakes (hot!)
handful of red chilies for garnish (optional)
1 medium red onion, cut into wedges
1 clove of garlic, roughly cut
four medium potatoes, peeled and cut into long quarters. (Use more if you like.)
2 whole fresh tomatoes, roughly chopped
1 fresh sprig of oregano
freshly ground black pepper
½ cup of water
olive oil
flour for dredging

METHOD
≡ Soak the baccalà for approx. 3 days, changing the water three time a day. Drain and set aside. Cut fillets into 2-inch pieces. Dredge in the flour. In a large fry pan, with a good lid, fry the fish a few minutes in olive oil until slightly brown. Remove fish from pan and set aside. Brown the red onion wedges in the pan. Add the potatoes and brown. Add the remaining ingredients and scrape the bottom of the pan to loosen all the browned bits. Place the fish on top and cover. Cook over very low heat for about half an hour. About half way through the cooking, uncover, and give everything a gentle toss. Return the lid and finish cooking.

- To serve: place on a serving dish and scatter some fresh parsley, and the fresh red chillies, if desired, for added colour.

Not for kids. Unless they have a hot tooth like our granddaughter Mistica once had when she was four.

This beautiful miraculous kid even scared me. She liked eating whole anchovies.

She kept a bottle of water in one hand while she ate my hot barbecue ribs with the other, telling me, between bites, 'I like it, but it's hot!' Then she drank the water. *Sigh.*

Love at first bite.

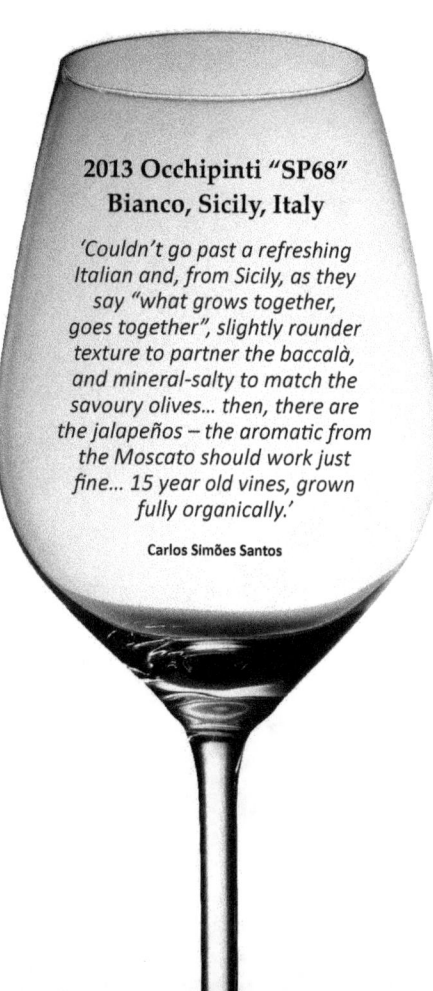

2013 Occhipinti "SP68" Bianco, Sicily, Italy

'Couldn't go past a refreshing Italian and, from Sicily, as they say "what grows together, goes together", slightly rounder texture to partner the baccalà, and mineral-salty to match the savoury olives... then, there are the jalapeños – the aromatic from the Moscato should work just fine... 15 year old vines, grown fully organically.'

Carlos Simões Santos

*I hate the opera.
I think I must have a tin ear.
No matter how hard I concentrate,
it still sounds like a bunch
of Italian chefs screaming
RISOTTO recipes at each other.*

Aristotle Onassis

Risotto di Zucca
(Pumpkin risotto, served in a whole pumpkin)

INGREDIENTS

2 tbsp olive oil
90 g butter
1 sprig rosemary, or parsley, finely chopped
1 garlic clove, whole
1 small pumpkin
300 g Carnaroli, Ferron or Aborio rice
small onion, finely diced
1 litre chicken stock, kept simmering, as needed, (or pumpkin stock, made from the pumpkin and onion scraps)
50 g parmesan cheese
salt and pepper
white wine or champagne

METHOD

- Prepare the whole pumpkin serving bowl. Carefully cut the top section out to make a lid, and de-seed. Hollow out enough of the flesh to accommodate the amount of risotto being served. (Reserve the seeds to roast later - to eat with salt.) You do not have to remove too much pumpkin. Take care not to puncture the skin. Cook the pumpkin flesh in the chicken stock, adding an optional chicken stock cube (or make a vegetable stock). Strain the stock and remove the pumpkin flesh. Keep the stock on simmer. Mash the cooked pumpkin and set aside.

- In pan, heat butter or olive oil and fry onion until soft, add rice and stir-fry for a few minutes. Add some white wine/champagne and cook for an additional two minutes. Add a little hot stock. Keep stirring at regular intervals. As the stock is absorbed, add more stock, a ladle at a time and stir in. When the rice has achieved al dente consistency, add the pumpkin. Continue to cook until rice is the way you like it. Remove from the heat and add the remaining butter and the Parmesan cheese. Cover and let rest for 10 minutes. Warm the inside of the pumpkin bowl with hot water, drain and pat dry. Fill with the risotto and sprinkle the chopped parsley or rosemary over the top. Place the lid back on (if desired) and serve with a dish of pesto on the side.

♪nOte: you can use the left-over pumpkin serving shell for soup or roast pumpkin.

Grapefruit Risotto
(served in a half grapefruit)

Remember with risotto: patience, and do not leave the pot unattended.

INGREDIENTS
1 grapefruit, cut in half for two bowls, and hollowed out.
1 extra grapefruit, juiced, and for 2 tbsp grated zest and some zest slivers.
1½ litres chicken stock
300 ml dry white wine
120 g unsalted butter
1 small onion, finely chopped
600 g Carnaroli, Ferron or Aborio rice
90 g parmesan cheese, finely grated
3 tbsp finely chopped fresh parsley

METHOD

- Hollow out a half grapefruit for each serving bowl, being careful not to puncture the skin. Set aside.
- Heat stock and wine in saucepan. In heavy fry pan, melt half butter over gentle heat and sauté onion until soft and translucent.
- Add rice and raise heat to moderate. Stir to ensure rice is evenly coated with butter.
- Add 1 cup of stock. Simmer, stirring constantly.
- Add a little hot stock whenever the liquid is absorbed, making sure the rice is just covered.
- After 15 - 20 minutes, remove risotto from the heat and taste rice. It should be perfectly cooked.
- Add cheese, remaining butter, and grapefruit zest and juice. Stir.
- Cover for two minutes.
- Fill each grapefruit half, sprinkle with parmesan cheese and garnish with parsley, some zest slivers and serve at once.

2020 Domaine Leflaive, Mâcon-Verzé 'Le Monte', Burgundy, France

'I am thinking that the risotto while rich, mouth filling and creamy, with grapefruit is also somehow refreshing... so is the wine, Domaine Leflaive is one of favourite producers from Burgundy for white wines... So a Chardonnay from the southern regions of Burgundy where generally riper fruit comes from, therefore the creaminess, richness in the wine to match naturally rich risotto... but then comes the tension of the wine, always strongly seen in Leflaive wines to bring freshness and parallel match the grapefruit.'

Carlos Simões Santos

Risotto Con Funghi in Flagrante Delicto

INGREDIENTS

1 stick celery, chopped finely
½ onion, pounded into a paste in a mortar and pestle
½ cup dried porcini mushrooms, soaked for a half hour and chopped finely
fresh rosemary
1 glass of dry white wine
500 g button mushrooms
1 litre vegetable stock
1 clove garlic, unpeeled
1 bay leaf
½ cup parmesan cheese
2 cups risotto rice (Carnaroli, Ferron or Aborio)
Olive oil
butter

METHOD

- To make a quick vegetable stock, place mixed vegetable scraps, cuttings and peelings into a litre of cold water. Add salt and pepper, a clove of unpeeled garlic and a bay leaf.

- Bring to a boil and cook for 15 minutes. Strain, return the stock to a clean pan and keep at a simmer while you're preparing the rice.

- Lightly sauté fresh mushrooms in grilling pan with salt, pepper, garlic and rosemary. Add some knobs of butter. Keep warm and set aside.

- Place 2 tbsp olive oil and 1 tbsp butter in pan. Add onion and celery and sauté for a few minutes until soft.

- Add rice and stir. Cook for one minute.

- Add white wine and cook for about a minute on high heat until alcohol evaporates.

- Added chopped porcini to the pot. Start adding hot stock, one ladle at a time to the pot over medium heat.

- Stir continuously. Do not leave unattended. When the rice is almost finished, add half the fresh mushrooms to the pot. Keep adding stock a little at a time until the rice is al dente.

- When the rice is cooked, stir in three tbsp of butter, the remaining mushrooms and the parmesan cheese and cover for ten minutes.

- Garnish with chopped parsley, parmesan cheese and black pepper.

Risi e Pisi con Finocchio Liberace
(Risotto with peas, fennel and… music)

Why don't I just step out and slip into something more spectacular?
Liberace

INGREDIENTS

1 bulb fennel, sliced in thick fillets
50 g butter
¼ cup dried porcini or shitake mushrooms, soaked in warm water for 15 minutes, drained and chopped finely
50 g parmesan cheese, freshly grated
2 cups Carnaroli, Ferron or Aborio rice
1 punnet fresh peas, shelled
5 cups light chicken stock, kept at a simmer
100 ml white wine
salt and pepper
finely chopped feathery fennel green tips

1 long playing Liberace record
1 candelabra (optional, but not really!)

METHOD

- Place the rice and the wine in a pot, bring to a boil, and cook until alcohol evaporates.
- Gradually add the hot stock to the rice, a ladle at a time, stirring continuously until it is absorbed, do not leave it unattended.
- Cook the fresh peas separately until firm but tender. Lightly sauté the fennel slices in a little butter.
- Set aside and keep warm.
- When the rice is ready, and al dente, remove from the heat, stir in the butter, parmesan cheese, and the peas, and place the fennel slices on top, cover the pot and let rest for five minutes.

to serve:

Plate with finely chopped feathery fennel green tips and freshly ground black pepper sprinkled over and thin shavings of parmesan cheese. Put on the Liberace record, light the candelabra, turn off the lights, and pour some wine.

Arancini
(Two-ways, with Mozzarella & Sweet Potato)

INGREDIENTS

2 cups left-over risotto, chilled
flour, seasoned with salt and pepper
small saucer of pasta sauce
2-3 eggs
dried bread crumbs, seasoned with chopped parsley
mozzarella, cut into small ¼ inch cubes
sweet potato, cooked until just tender, cut into small ¼ inch cubes
oil for frying

METHOD

- Have a small bowl of water handy to moisten your hands while you work.
- Scoop up a half-cup or so of rice, flatten it in your palm, and place a mozzarella cube in the centre, and a tsp of tomato sauce.
- Fold the rice over onto itself and pat and roll into a small ball. Moisten your hands further if necessary to keep the rice from sticking.
- Pat the balls firmly and set aside.
- Do the same with the sweet potato cubes, only omit the tomato sauce.
- Beat the eggs into a flat bowl and put the bread crumbs in another flat dish.
- Dip the ball in the egg and then roll them in the breadcrumbs.
- Place a half-inch of oil in the pan and heat until just smoking.
- Remove from heat and put the rice balls in the oil, turning them.
- Place the pan back on the heat and fry the balls until golden.
- Keep an eye on the heat and remove the pan from the heat if necessary to insure they don't burn and cook evenly.
- Drain on paper towels and serve.

Sweet Potato Gnocchi
w/ Sage Leaves, Brown Butter & Guanciale

I love being able to get a second meal out of the left-overs of the first meal. Well, not precisely left-overs, in the strict sense, as we are planning this second dish when we prepare the first. The key is making more than you need the first time. So double or triple the recipe.

Ideal dishes to do this with are any white rice dish (which gives us congee the next day), risotto (which gives us arancini) and mashed potatoes (in this case, sweet potatoes, which gives us gnocchi.)

INGREDIENTS
1 cup of left-over cooked sweet potato, chilled
flour
1 egg
fresh sage leaves
butter
four slices of guanciale
salt and pepper

METHOD
- Mix the sweet potato, some flour, salt and pepper and the egg together until you have a very light sticky dough.
- Turn onto a floured board and start to work the mass into a long thin cigar shape, adding flour a little at a time, until it just holds together. Do not over-flour or the gnocchi will be too heavy. With a sharp knife, cut the long roll into bite-sized pieces.
- Lightly dust the gnocchi with flour and set aside or put in the refrigerator until ready to use.
- Bring a pot of water to the boil and tip in the gnocchi. Simmer until they rise to the surface at which point they are cooked.
- Put a little olive oil in a medium pan and cook the guanciale until softened.
- Take out of pan and drain on paper towels, reserving the oil.
- Add some butter to the oil and the sage leaves until they start to wilt and the butter starts to brown slightly. Do not burn. Remove pan from heat.
- Drain the gnocchi and toss in the butter-sage mixture until well coated.
- Serve with the guanciale on top and some freshly grated black pepper and parmesan cheese.

Polenta
(soft & hard)

When I lived on the Star Mountain commune, in Northern California, back in the peace-and-love 70s, I made this dish, with a Napoli sauce, once a week for about 25 people who lived there with me. It was my weekly big family dish.

METHOD

- Add one part coarse or fine polenta to four parts cold water and bring to a boil.
- Reduce heat and simmer gently, stirring often until a wooden spoon stands up in the polenta unassisted.
- Add butter and salt.
- Serve hot with topping of choice.
- Tip the remainder of the polenta onto a wooden board and let cool.

It can now be sliced and fried in olive oil and served as above, or fried in butter, for breakfast, with maple syrup or honey.

Nasi Tumpeng w/ Satays & Choko-Chicken Kari

One of Indonesia's most festive dishes. For another presentation, you can position the rice cone, on a banana leaf, in the centre of a large platter and arrange a half dozen side dishes around it. This picture is from a family feast right after we returned from Bali where I learned to make it from a Balinese grandmother in a cooking class, in Ubud.

for the rice cone:

INGREDIENTS

1 kg long grain rice
80 ml oil
2 onions
3 garlic cloves, chopped
2 litres of coconut milk
1 tbsp salt
2 tsp turmeric
6 dried daun salam leaves or 2 pandanus leaves (if you can't find either, a drop of vanilla essence and a kaffir lime leaf is a good substitute)
banana leaves to serve
2 Lebanese cucumbers, thickly sliced
3 bird's eye chillis, seeded and sliced
3 green chilles, seeded and sliced

METHOD

- Wash the rice and drain.
- Let rest for half hour.
- Heat oil in large saucepan with a lid over low heat.
- Add the onion and garlic and cook for a few minutes until onion is soft.
- Add the rice and stir for 2-3 minutes
- Add the coconut milk, salt, turmeric and the leaves (or vanilla and kaffir lime leaf).
- Bring to a boil and stir well.
- Reduce to low heat, cover and steam 20 minutes.
- When finished, stir in any coconut milk gathered on the side of pot, replace lid and continue over low heat for another 2 minutes.
- Remove from heat, uncover and allow to cool a little.

- Remove the seasoning leaves and turn the rice on to a large platter lined with washed banana leaves.
- Shape into a cone using a cone-shaped mould (a funnel works!) or an oiled banana leaf.
- Arrange the accompaniments around the cone, if desired, or serve as side dishes.

garnish:

Make a flower with one of the chilis. Scrap out the seeds, cut off the stem end and make some slits above the tip to the stem end. Put in some ice water and the strips will curl up. Put this on top of the cone. You can also make a little cap out of foil or banana leaf, secure with a toothpick and use this to cap the cone.

Balinese Choko-Chicken Kari
w/ Kaffir Lime & Leaves

Commonly referred to as 'curry', a South Asian scholar, Ilyse Morgenstein Furest Ph.D, believes that term came from a 'British bad ear' during colonial times. I'm using the traditional Tami spelling - which simply means sauce.

Chokos fascinate me. I read once in the late poet Robert Adamson's memoir that he loved chokos with butter as a kid. When I invited the poet Les Murray AO over for dinner and asked him if there was anything he didn't eat, he said, 'I eat everything… except chokos.'

INGREDIENTS

2 chokos, potatoes or green papaya – or a mixture - peeled and cored, and cut into one-inch pieces
2 boneless chicken thighs, cut into one-inch pieces
1 onion, chopped finely
1 tsp coriander seeds
1 tsp cumin seeds
½ tsp black peppercorns
1 tsp black mustard seeds
2 tbsp fresh kari leaves
1 level tbsp turmeric
1 tbsp palm sugar (or raw sugar)
½ red bird's eye chilli, chopped finely
2 cloves garlic, chopped roughly
1 inch piece of ginger, grated
2 kaffir lime leaves, slightly crushed
1 whole kaffir lime, quartered.
1 piece lemongrass, pounded and tied in a knot
1 small can coconut milk
1 tsp salt
oil for frying

METHOD

- Toast coriander, cumin seeds and peppercorns in a small skillet. Grind in a mortar & pestle.
- Brown chicken pieces in some oil. Remove and set aside
- Add mustard seeds and kari leaves to oil – sauté 5 minutes.
- Add onion and sauté until clear.
- Add garlic, ginger and chile - sauté five minutes.

- Add ground spices and turmeric – sauté five minutes.
- Add choko, potatoes or green papaya – stir until well-coated.
- Return chicken pieces to skillet. Combine.
- Add enough water to just cover. Add kaffir lime leaves, kaffir lime and lemongrass.
- Bring to simmer. Cover and simmer 20 minutes over low heat.
- Add coconut milk and sugar. Cook another 15 minutes to combine flavours, or until vegetables are tender.
- Check seasoning.
- Serve on steamed rice, garnished with peanuts and fresh coriander.

Beef & Chicken Satays
(w/Two Sauces)

INGREDIENTS
2 chicken breasts or thighs, deboned, and cut into bite-size pieces
1 onion, cut into small bite-sized pieces
½ bell pepper (capsicum) any colour
8 satay sticks, soaked in water
1 clove garlic, chopped finely
½ inch ginger, grated
1 small chili, chopped finely
soy sauce
kecap manis
water
olive oil
salt and pepper

METHOD

- Make a marinade with the garlic, ginger, chili, soy sauce, kecap manis and water in any combination you wish. Place the chicken pieces in the marinade to cover, and leave, covered, overnight in the fridge.

- Next day, soak the satay sticks in water for about an hour before using (keeps them from burning too fast) and make the two sauces.

peanut sauce:

INGREDIENTS
½ cup peanut butter
¼ cup water
soy sauce
garlic, minced
ginger, grated
red chili, sliced finely
coconut milk
olive oil or coconut oil

METHOD

- Place a little oil in a pan and add the garlic, ginger and chili. Stir for one minute. Add the water and the peanut butter and stir until it starts to become smooth. Add coconut milk to thin it to the consistency you like. Keep warm.

kecap manis sauce:

INGREDIENTS
**kecap manis
¼ cup water
garlic, minced
ginger, grated
red chili, sliced finely**

METHOD

- Place a little oil in a pan and add the garlic, ginger and chilli. Stir for one minute. Add the water and the kecap manis and stir until it starts to become smooth. Add water and/or more kecap manis to thin it to the consistency you like. Keep warm.
- Thread the chicken pieces and the onion and bell pepper pieces alternately onto the satay sticks and set aside.
- Add some more soy sauce, kecap manis and water to the marinade and use this to baste the satays while they are grilling.
- Heat a bbq or a stove-top grill pan to smoking, brush with a little oil and put the satay sticks on the grill. Turn and baste frequently until done.
- To serve, place the satay sticks on a serving plate and drizzle the two sauces over top.

Cashew Nut Kari

This is the dish I made for Lin van Hek on our first date in 1980! (She must have liked it because we're still together after 43 years.)

INGREDIENTS

3 cups thin coconut milk
1 cup thick coconut milk
1 medium onion, finely sliced
2 fresh green chillies, seeded and chopped
½ teas ground turmeric
2 cloves garlic, finely chopped
½ teas fresh ginger, finely grated
2 inch stick of cinnamon
4 pieces dried daun pandan leaf (or substitute 1 drop vanilla essence and 1 small kaffir lime leaf)
1 stalk lemon grass or two strips of lemon rind
8 kari leaves
250 g raw cashew nuts
salt to taste

METHOD

≡ Put all ingredients, except nuts, salt and thick coconut milk, into a large saucepan and simmer gently uncovered for 10 minutes. Add cashew nuts and salt and cook gently for approx. 30 minutes or until cashew nuts are tender. Add thick coconut milk and simmer 5 minutes longer. Serve with rice, chutneys, pickles, Thai chilli sauce and fresh coriander leaves.

Serves two naïve kids.
Left-overs will last forever.

2019 Eitelsbacher Karthäuserhof, Riesling, Kabinett, Mosel, Germany

'I feel like this dish has creaminess enough, slight sweet and curried spices, but also herbal... so I am thinking of a lovely German classic! One of the oldest monasteries in the country – 1335! Vineyards were planted for over 400 years here... Gently off dry to pair the coconut sweetness, high acidity to rinse the fattiness of the milk, and floral, fragrant and perfumed to refresh the palate from spices. Confident about this one.'

Carlos Simões Santos

Potato Kari

INGREDIENTS

2 potatoes, white and/or sweet, peeled and cut in fine slices,
soaked in cold water to keep from discolouration
1 medium onion, finely diced
2 tbsp black mustard seeds
1 tbsp turmeric powder
5 tbsp kari leaves
2 tbsp freshly ground coriander
1 tbsp freshly ground cumin power
½ teas red chilli flakes (or fresh red chilli, sliced)
2 cloves garlic, chopped finely
1 inch piece of fresh ginger, chopped finely
safflower or peanut oil
milk to cover
2 tbsp butter (or ghee)
salt and black pepper

METHOD

- Heat oil and butter (or ghee) in pan. Do not allow butter to burn.
- Add mustard seeds and kari leaves and cook for a couple of minutes. Add the chilli flakes (or fresh chilli) and the onions and sauté a couple minutes until soft. Add the garlic and ginger and sauté for one minute.
- Add the ground spices and fry for 2 minutes.
- Add the sliced potatoes and sweet potatoes and stir until they are coated in the spices and bright yellow.
- Add enough milk to just barely cover the potatoes. Bring to the boil. Cover and reduce to a simmer on low heat and cook until potatoes are tender, about 15 minutes.
- Stir once during cooking. Add salt and pepper to taste.

To cook the rice

- Wash 1 cup of rice.
- Add it to 2 cups of water in a pan, and let stand for 30 minutes. Bring the rice to a boil, cover, reduce to very low and cook for approx. 15 minutes. Check to see if the rice is tender. If so, turn off the heat, leave covered and let rest for another ten minutes. If the rice isn't tender, cook for another 5 minutes, and then turn off the heat and let rest.

garnishes:

INGREDIENTS

1 lime leaf, shaved very finely
½ cup of peanuts, roasted until golden in a frying pan,
medium grind in a mortar and pestle,
with a little salt added
sweet mango chutney
hot lime pickle, with oil
yogurt, with fresh banana slices cut into it
fresh basil, Vietnamese basil and coriander leaves

to serve:

METHOD

- Use a large plate.
- Place about a cup of rice into a cup, press firmly and then turn the moulded rice into the centre of the plate.
- Spoon some kari over the rice and garnish with basil, Vietnamese basil and coriander leaves. Scatter some of the crushed peanuts around the plate.
- Dot about ten drops of the lime pickle oil carefully on the plate for an attractive presentation. (You can also sprinkle some of the crushed peanuts on the yogurt-banana side dish.)

Green Cabbage Kari

INGREDIENTS

half green cabbage, shredded finely.
half onion, chopped finely.
1 tsp brown mustard seeds
handful of kari leaves
1 clove of garlic, chopped roughly
1-inch piece of ginger, grated
1 tbsp coriander, ground
1 tbsp cumin, ground
1 teas turmeric, ground
2 tbsp oil or ghee
salt

METHOD

- Heat the oil and add the mustard seeds and kari leaves until the seeds pop. Watch the leaves do not burn.

- Add the onion and sauté. Add the garlic and ginger and stir for one minute, careful not to burn the garlic. Add the three spices and stir for a couple of minutes. Add the cabbage, salt to taste, a tbsp of water and cover. Simmer over low heat until cabbage is cooked. Garnish with fresh coriander.

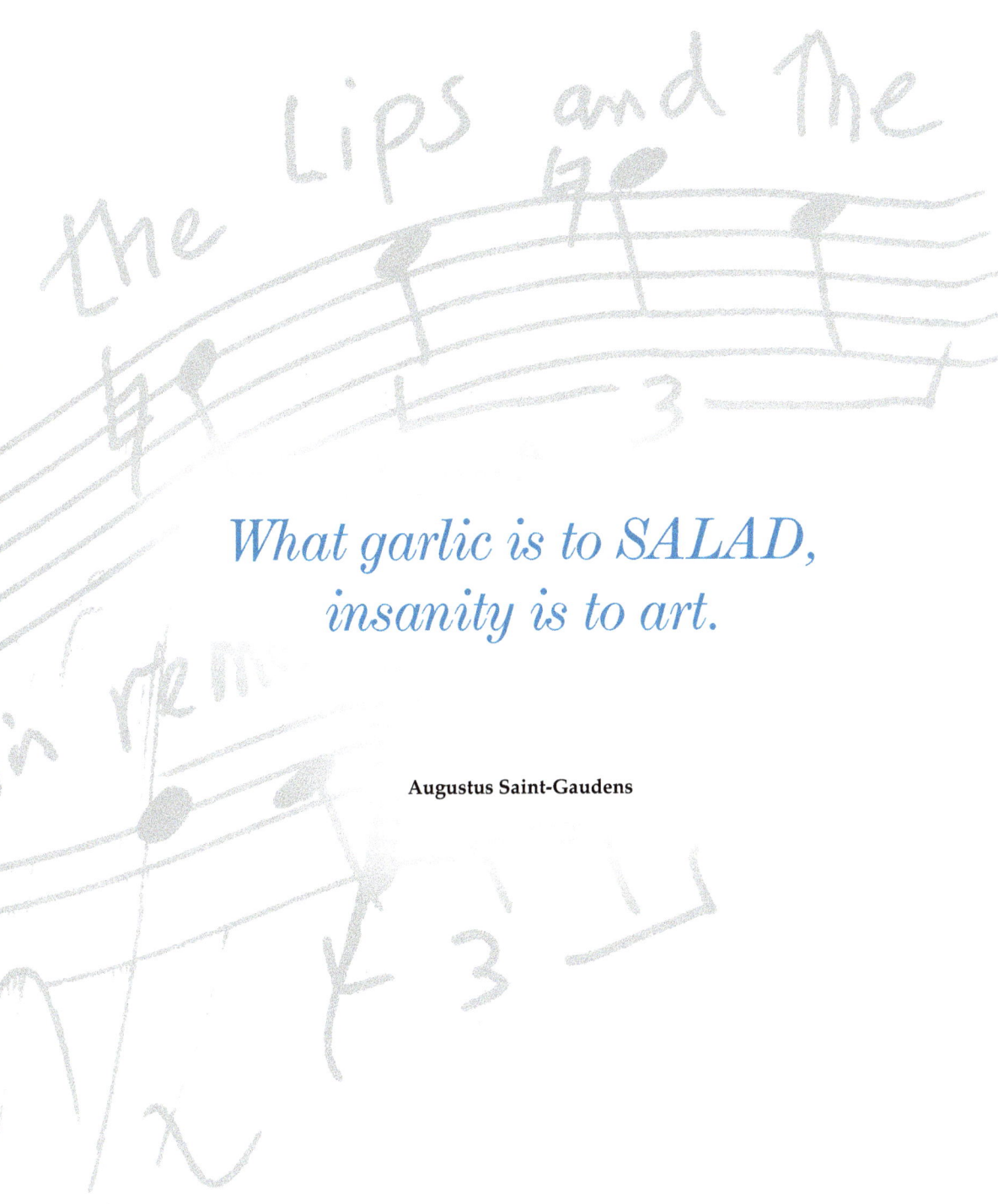

What garlic is to SALAD, insanity is to art.

Augustus Saint-Gaudens

Watermelon, Spinach & Feta Salad

I learned this from our daughter-in-law, Danni Zanetti.
She makes hers with fresh basil instead of young spinach leaves.

salad:

INGREDIENTS

fresh watermelon, cut into chunks
small spinach leaves, washed and spun dry
feta cheese, in small cubes
red onion, sliced thinly

dressing:

balsamic vinegar
olive oil
salt and pepper

METHOD

≡ Mix all salad ingredients together.

≡ Dress with balsamic and oil.

≡ Season to taste.

North Vietnamese Kohlrabi Salad
(Nộm su hào)

I learned this dish from Chef Nguyễn Mạnh Chiến.

INGREDIENTS
½ kohlrabi, peeled
½ carrot, peeled
caster sugar
white or apple cider vinegar
sesame seeds, toasted
peanuts, crushed
fresh coriander
½ small red chili, sliced (optional)

garnish:

½ red bell pepper or capsicum (optional)
¼ red onion, thinly sliced (optional)
shredded chicken (optional)

METHOD
- Shred the kohlrabi finely, salt freely and let rest for 20 minutes.
- Squeeze out as much liquid as you can from the grated kohlrabi.
- Shred the carrot finely and place in a bowl with the kohlrabi and red chili.
- The ratio should be 90% kohlrabi to 10% carrot.
- Season with a little vinegar, a sprinkle of sugar, crushed nuts, seeds and chili to taste.
- Garnish with coriander leaves.

Potato & Pumpkin Salad

INGREDIENTS

600 g scrubbed Kipfler potatoes, peeled or unpeeled
100 g pumpkin
½ apple, peeled and chopped
2 tbsp chopped preserved lemon rind
1 tbsp wholegrain mustard
2 tbsp lemon juice
½ cup whole-egg mayonnaise
1 stick celery, chopped
chives or parsley, finely chopped
sea salt, freshly cracked black pepper, sweet paprika

METHOD

- Cook the scrubbed potatoes in boiling water until tender.
- Rinse under cold water and cut into medium cubes. Let cool slightly.
- Do the same with the pumpkin, only cut into smaller cubes.
- Mix everything together in a bowl and toss.
- You can also add some fresh roquette leaves (arugula).
- Chill or serve warm.

Peace & Love Salad

You can figure this one out for yourselves! Ad libitum!

Assertive French Salad Dressing

INGREDIENTS

anchovies and garlic, minced and mashed
Dijon mustard
red wine vinegar
salt, a pinch
black pepper, ground
pancetta or bacon, just the reduced fat (reserve the crispy bits and chop)
olive oil

METHOD

≡ Dress the salad with a ratio of 4 parts oil to 1 part vinegar. Not too wet.

♪nOte: garnish with boiled eggs, croutons or crispy pancetta bits.

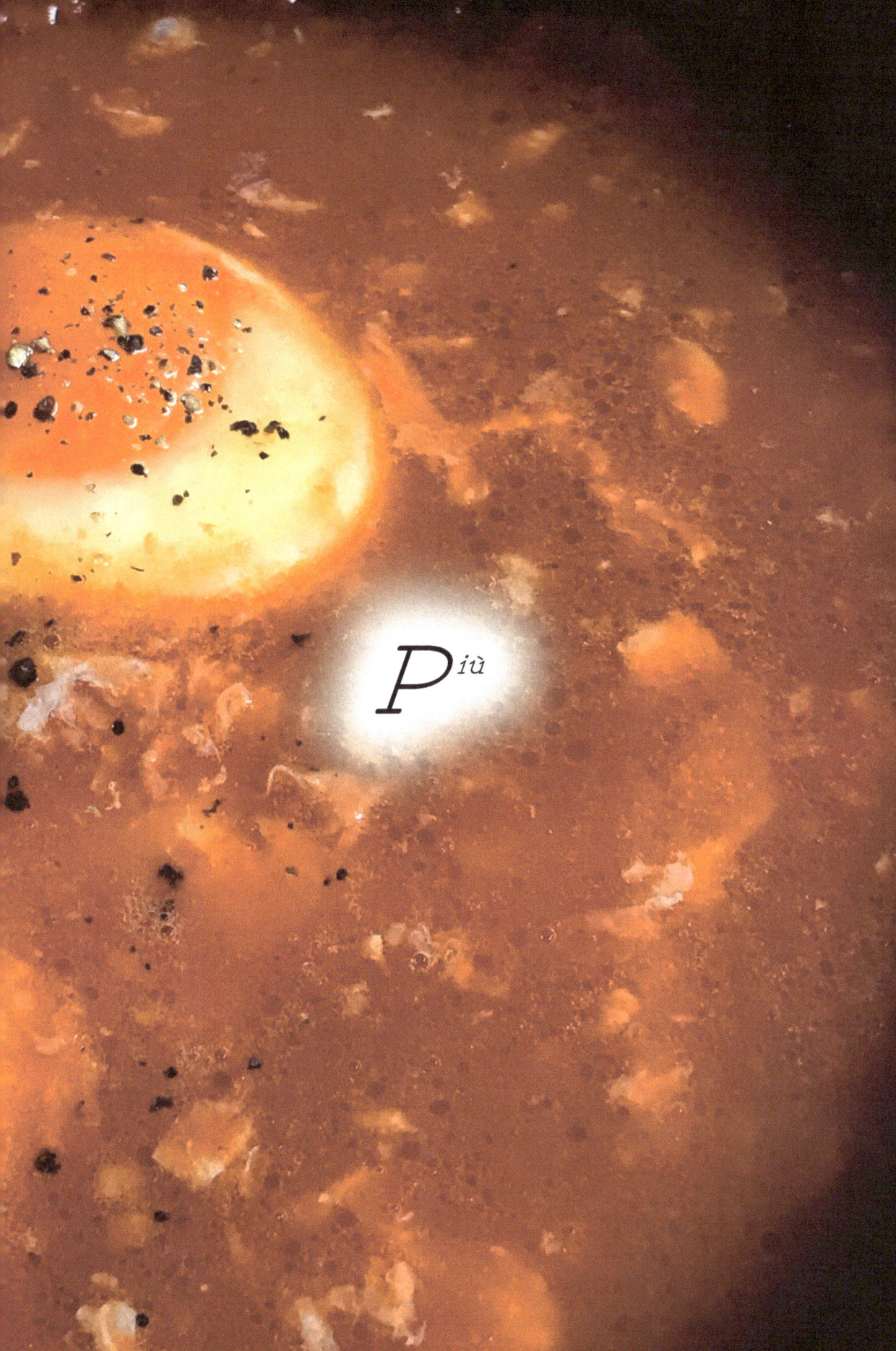

Fried Green Tomatoes, w/Guanciale

The inspiration for this came from the magical film, *Fried Green Tomatoes at the Whistle Stop Café*.

The guanciale is my Italian-roots contribution.

INGREDIENTS

4 large green tomatoes
2 eggs
½ cup milk
½ cup flour
½ cup fine cornmeal
½ cup bread crumbs
2 teaspoons coarse kosher salt
¼ teaspoon ground black pepper
¼ teaspoon cayenne pepper
guanciale, chopped into small chunks (or substitute pancetta or bacon

METHOD

- Slice tomatoes ½ inch thick. Discard the ends.
- Whisk eggs and milk together in a medium-size bowl.
- Scoop flour onto a plate. Mix cornmeal, bread crumbs and salt and pepper on another plate. Dip tomatoes into flour to coat. Then dip the tomatoes into milk and egg mixture. Dredge in breadcrumbs to completely coat.
- Put in the fridge for 15 minutes.
- In a large skillet, fry the guanciale until the fat is rendered (enough so that there is ¼ inch of fat in the pan) - remove the crispy chunks and set aside.
- Place tomatoes into the frying pan in batches of 4 or 5, depending on the size of your skillet. Do not crowd the tomatoes, they should not touch each other. When the tomatoes are browned, flip and fry them on the other side.
- Drain them on paper towels. Serve with the crispy bits on top and hot sauce on the side.

You can also omit the cornmeal and just dust in flour and fry.

Egg Foo Yung
w/ Sausage Gravy

I first ate this dish in a Chinese restaurant when I lived in Cambridge, Mass, when I was 22 years old. I was in a band, at the time, called *The Headstone Circus*. I used to love to spend a lot of daytime hours sitting under the trees, on the Cambridge University common, writing unrequited love poems - and I would have Egg Foo Yung for lunch about three times a week, to help ease my heartache, I guess. I have never had it anywhere since. Just the other day, the recipe came back to me, complete in every detail. I prepared it, and it tasted exactly the way I remembered. Maybe all that lost love has finally been requited.

INGREDIENTS
500 g of mung bean sprouts
4 eggs, beaten
2 spring onions, finely sliced on the diagonal
1 chicken breast
1 Italian pork sausage, casing removed, and minced with a fork
some chicken stock
2 tbsp flour
½ onion, finely chopped
fresh parsley and coriander, finely chopped
1 shitake mushroom, chopped finely and sautéed in a little butter
olive oil for frying
salt & pepper

METHOD

- Make a little chicken stock for the gravy: fresh or with a stock cube.
- Cut up the chicken breast in medium size pieces and simmer in water until the chicken is soft enough to break apart.
- Remove the chicken from the stock and set the stock aside. When the chicken is cool enough to handle, tear into fine shreds.
- Mix the chicken, bean sprouts, eggs, spring onions, fresh herbs, mushrooms and the salt and pepper together to make a chunky omelette batter.
- Rest in the fridge while you make the gravy.

Sausage Gravy

METHOD

- Place some oil in a pan and when hot, cook the onions until soft. Add the sausage mince and fry. When the mince is cooked, remove from pan and set aside. Add flour to the pan fat and cook for a minute. Slowly add the stock until you have smooth gravy. Add more water if necessary. Return the mince to the pan, season to taste, and stir over low heat. Keep adding just enough water to keep the gravy smooth and when it's ready, remove from the heat while you cook the Egg Foo Yung patties.

- Place a little olive oil in a skillet, and when it is hot, add enough of the omelette mixture to make 3-4 medium sized patties. When they are golden on one side, flip over and cook on the other side.

- Place two patties on a plate and spoon the sausage gravy over the top, with fresh coriander on the side.

Flemish-style Tossed Potatoes w/ Dill

These go nicely with the schnitzels. The dish comes from Lin van Hek's life when she lived in Belgium and cooked, in exchange for room and board, for an old Flemish farmer and his two sons.

INGREDIENTS
ten small potatoes, peeled or unpeeled
1½ cloves garlic, chopped finely
butter
fresh dill, some finely chopped, and keep some whole for the garnish
salt & pepper

METHOD

- Boil the potatoes until cooked.
- Drain the water.
- Add butter, garlic, salt and pepper, and chopped dill to the whole potatoes in the pan, and place the lid on the pan.
- Give the pan a good shake so that the potatoes come apart slightly.

Cookbooks for poets

Ann Rogers' *Poor Poet's Cookbook* -
a nickel dinner, fresh roll,
real butter, and a glass of wine,
Onion Pie, Black Beans and Rum.
Inspired by Mary Randolph's, *The Virginia Housewife*, 1824 -
curry of catfish, barbequed shoat & beaten biscuits,
fried calf's feet, pheasant a-la-daub,
tansy pudding, pickled nasturtiums, walnut catsup,
vinegar of the four thieves.
The food and customs of the antebellum South.
A culinary pantheon that included Alice B. Toklas,
Fannie Farmer and M.F.K Fisher's,
How to Cook a Wolf, 1942 -
the latter, written to inspire courage,
in those daunted by wartimes shortages.
W.H Auden, of Fisher, remarked -
'I do not know of anyone in the United States
who writes better prose.'
John Updike added -
'Poet of the appetites'.

Eggs Obstáculos

INGREDIENTS
2 tbsp butter
¾ cup salsa piquante, or tomato sauce with a tsp of favourite hot sauce
4 eggs
½ cup beer of choice
toast, buttered
salt & black pepper

METHOD

- Heat butter in small saucepan.
- Add sauce and bring to simmer.
- Make the toast.
- Break eggs into sauce and turn down heat.
- When eggs are cooked, tip beer in and serve with toast.

This comes from a classic 1942 cookbook titled *How To Cook a Wolf*, by MFK Fisher. Allegedly invented by a young Mexican painter.

Obstáculo means obstacle, impediment or constraint. The latter half of the word contains a reference to something well-known by Italians and the Spanish but I can find no etymological basis for assuming that overtone, unless of course, you use too much hot sauce.

The title of the book and the recipes come from post-depression years so I would think it references the idea that even in difficult times, you can eat well.

Apologizes to Carlos here:

As well as wine sommeliers, there are also sake sommeliers, milk sommeliers, water sommeliers and even beer sommeliers, the latter also known as cicerones. The word cicerone come from the name of Marcus 'Tully' Cicero, the Roman orator, and refers to someone having the eloquence and learning of Cicero. As an aspiring cicerone, I would like to food-beer pair this dish with:

Coopers Brewery Longneck Red Sparkling Ale 5.8%

My mate, Bruscia Mechanicus Pittsus, who used to work on our old 80s Holden, before it spit the dummus, assures me that the longnecks are far superior in taste to the stubbies due to the sediment being left in the bottle.

Josephus Ludovicus Dulci

Poached Eggs in Milk on Toast w/Nutmeg

This was one of my mom's signature breakfast dishes. I have never seen it anywhere else.

INGREDIENTS
1 egg
cup of milk
buttered toast
grated nutmeg
salt and pepper

METHOD

- Toast the bread. Put the milk in a saucepan.
- Break the egg gently into the milk and poach until cooked.
- Butter the toast and spoon the egg and as much milk as you like over the top.
- Sprinkle some nutmeg over and salt and pepper to taste.

Eggs-Over-Easy
w/ Italian Sausage, Jalapeños & Red-Eye Gravy

INGREDIENTS
2 Italian sausages
2 eggs
freshly brewed coffee
butter
olive oil
home-made bbq sauce (from ribs recipe)

METHOD

- Two pans, one for the eggs and one for the sausages.
- Brew some fresh coffee. Keep warm.
- Slice a couple fresh jalapeños into strips. (Leave the seeds and membranes if you want the dish hot - remove them, if you want it mild.)
- Break up the sausages into one-inch pieces and fry until about half done. Then add the jalapeños and fry until ready.
- Fry the eggs over easy in butter and season with salt and pepper.

- Plate the eggs, sausages & peppers.
- Add some BBQ sauce to the sausage pan and a ½ cup of coffee.
- Remove from heat and stir until thickened slightly.
- Serve over eggs and sausages.

Poached Eggs in Milk on Toast

Lemonscent

The lane neglected in leaf and wrapper
non-descript off the main
save fruit-laden branches peering
over grey board
the old tree stopped me dead
I detoured in pulling the nearest down
snapping the stem others were higher than reach
while looking for something to lift me
I recalled civil law on harvesting fruit
overhanging public lanes: property of owner
still sour sunfaces and green-yellow leers
can't be resisted sliding a wheelie bin balancing shakily
one hand on fence one arm stretching
into thorny light I barely tickled the bottom
rind of a fat one
as the back gate swung open
a lemon-haired woman invited me in
to pick all I wanted
I wouldn't want you to get scratches
helping fill my coat pockets
I like sharing
we touched hands briefly
thanks and goodbye
I left her pleasant lane
returning to a duller street
saturated with scent
of good tidings and lemon.

Annie's Preserved Lemons

I quote from Chef Annie Fiume:

I really don't have the recipe written down. As to quantities, I go by look and feel. But basically you cut the lemons into quarters. Scrub them clean first. Put them in a bowl and add coarse salt.

Probably at least a cup for about 5 or 6 lemons. Rub them all over with the salt. Then put them in the sterilized jar, layering with cinnamon sticks, bay leaves, cloves, peppercorns.

Pour all the salt in. Really squash them down to release some juice and pack them in. Put them in a cool, dark cupboard and invert every couple of days. You can use them after a month.

Nastro Azzurro Fried Onion Rings

INGREDIENTS
1 litre oil for deep frying
1 cup flour
1 cup cold Nastro Azzurro Italian beer
1 pinch of salt
1 pinch of ground black pepper
3-4 brown onions, peeled and sliced in ¼ inch slices
4 ice cubes

METHOD

- Place the ice cubes in the bottom of a bowl and pour in the cold beer. Stir in the flour, salt and pepper until a smooth batter forms. Let rest for a half hour or more.

- Separate the onions into individual rings (leave some bunched up for variety) and place in a separate bowl.

- In a large pot or fry pan, heat the oil until a drop of batter starts to sizzle.

- Put a handful of onion slices into the batter and coat thoroughly.

- Using the tongs, lift each onion ring out of the batter, shake a little and deep fry, five or six at a time, until golden. Leave enough room for them to move so they don't stick together. If they do, just separate them with two pairs of tongs. Remove and drain on paper towels.

- Salt and place in a serving bowl lined with a couple sheets of paper towels.

- Every other batch, remove the pan from the heat, to allow it to cool slightly, and with a slotted spoon remove the burnt bits of the batter so it stays clear.

- Place the pan back on the heat and repeat until all the onion slices are finished. Serve with lemon wedges and tartar sauce.

♪nOte: The beer has enough yeast in it to create a thin perfect tempura-like batter. It is not necessary to add eggs or baking powder.

Roast Garlic Hummus

METHOD

- If using dried chickpeas, cover with cold water and leave overnight.
- Drain the chickpeas and transfer to a clean pot and add cold water to cover.
- Add in 1 tsp of baking soda.
- Bring to a boil over high heat and then simmer for 30-40 minutes over low heat.
- Drain, reserving some of the water, and transfer chickpeas to a clean bowl.
- Cover with cold water.
- If you want a creamier hummus, place your hands in the water and rub off and remove as many of the skins as you can.
- (You don't have to do this with canned chick peas which also do not require overnight soaking.)

INGREDIENTS

roasted garlic oil

METHOD

- cook 1 ½ cups of garlic cloves in 2 cups of extra virgin olive oil, over very low heat, for 30-40 minutes or until soft and very browned.

INGREDIENTS

4 cups of cooked dried chickpeas or 4 ½ cups canned
½ cup tahini
juice of 1 lemon
⅓ cup roasted garlic
¼ cup roasted garlic olive
sea salt and cayenne pepper to taste

METHOD

- Add the chickpeas to a blender and pulse into a thick paste. You may have to stir in a little soaking water to keep it moving.
- Add the tahini, lemon juice, garlic, and salt.
- Blend 5 minutes while drizzling in the roasted garlic olive oil.
- Add more of any ingredients to taste as you wish.

Serve with a splash of olive oil, cayenne, and chopped parsley.

Elegy for old feller

The little old bloke nose like a tomato
from too much grog has vanished
scrawny in his slept-in clothes
he walked an even scrawnier dog
past our house for years
muttering at the unseen
I never spoke to him except once
to invite him to a neighbourly block
barbeque out on the nature strip
come over and have a sausage, I said.
Naw, I don't eat foreign food.

Breaded Silverbeet Stalks

When I was a kid, in Painesville, Ohio, my Sicilian grandmother used to make this with cardoons, a thistle-like plant that grew as a weed she picked down by the railroad tracks. My daughter Brea made this for me recently with silverbeet stalks and it brought back some memories.

INGREDIENTS
Swiss chard or silverbeet stalks, cut into four inch pieces
dried bread crumbs
egg
olive oil or safflower oil, enough to deep fry
salt & pepper to taste
parmesan cheese, grated

METHOD

- Place the stalks from the silverbeet (Swiss chard) into a pot of water, bring to the boil and simmer until tender, about 15-20 minutes.
- Place fresh bread crumbs in a dish, and the beaten egg in another.
- Heat the oil until a small piece of bread sizzles in it.
- Drain the stalks, dip in the beaten egg and then in the bread crumbs.
- Deep fry in small batches and drain on paper towels. Season with salt and pepper.

(This can also be baked in the oven.)

Serve with **Yogurt-Garlic Sauce**.

Chile Rellenos

INGREDIENTS
6 large poblano peppers
1 cup cheddar cheese, shredded
½ inch oil
3 eggs
½ tsp salt

METHOD

- Place poblanos over open flame on stove and blacken them.
- Put in a plastic bag to sweat for five minutes. Scrape the skin off gently with a knife, keeping them intact.
- Split them down side, from the tip, without cutting through, to make a pocket. Remove the seeds and membranes with your fingers without tearing.
- Carefully stuff the peppers with the cheese. Gently close the opening of the peppers and secure with toothpicks. Set aside.
- Heat oil in a large saucepan over medium. Prepare batter. Separate the egg whites from the yolks into two bowls. Beat the whites until stiff peaks form. Gently fold in the egg whites one at a time until all of them are fully mixed in but do not stir.
- Place flour and salt onto plate. Roll the stuffed poblanos in the flour, then give them a tap to remove any excess. Dip them in the egg batter and place them in the hot oil. Fry for 4 minutes per side, until golden brown. Don't crowd them or they will be greasy.
- Transfer to paper towels to drain. Remove the toothpicks and serve with some salsa and freshly chopped coriander.

salsa:

INGREDIENTS
6 tomatoes, chopped
½ small onion, chopped
3 cloves garlic, chopped
1 jalapeño de-seeded (leave the seeds in if you like a little pain)
5 sprigs fresh coriander
1 tsp salt
1 tsp olive oil

METHOD

- Add tomatoes, onion, garlic, jalapeño, coriander and salt to a blender. Purée until smooth. Heat olive oil in a pan. Add salsa and bring to a boil. Simmer over low heat for 8 minutes.
- Season to taste.

DOLCE e con affetto

Inzuppare il biscotto
(Italian: to soak the biscuit, ie. to have sex)

Who could resist

that Butternut Snap lap

crumbly like an

Anzac in the sack

Scotch Finger steady

on the Tiny Teddy

Swallow's Bush Biscuit

Milk Arrowroot and

Adora Cream lips breathlessly

mumblin' the

Honey Jumble?

Kama Sutra Chocolate Tart

chocolate pastry:

INGREDIENTS
125 g chilled unsalted butter
1 tbsp caster sugar
200 g plain flour
2 tbsp Dutch cocoa
2 egg yolks

filling:

INGREDIENTS
300 g dark couverture chocolate, finely chopped
100 ml double cream
125 g unsalted butter, chopped
4 eggs
100 g caster sugar
1 tbsp golden syrup

METHOD

- Cream butter, sugar, flour and cocoa powder until the mix resembles coarse breadcrumbs. Add egg yolks and 1 ½ tbsp iced water and continue mixing only until just combined. The dough might still be a little sticky. Wrap in plastic wrap and chill for at least an hour. Knead the chilled dough lightly first to soften, then roll out evenly in all directions with a small amount of dusting powder.

Blind bake:

- Line a 3.5 cm deep, 24 cm fluted tart tin, with a removable bottom, with the pastry, pressing gently into base and sides. Cut excess pastry around edge with rolling pin, cover with plastic wrap and chill the tart case for one hour. Preheat oven to 180°C. Press a layer of aluminium foil into the tart case and fill with pastry weights or dried beans to keep the edges stable in the oven. Bake for 10 -15 minutes. Remove from oven when outer edge of crust is cooked. Remove beans and check bottom. If bottom is still moist, return to oven (without beans) for five minutes until base is ready.

- For the filling, combine chocolate, cream and butter in a heatproof bowl over a saucepan of simmering water and stir continuously until butter and chocolate are melted and mixture is well combined. Remove bowl from heat and set aside. Whisk eggs, sugar and golden syrup until pale and creamy, then fold into chocolate mixture.

- Pour filling into tart shell.

Tip: Place a pizza pan, or any flat surfaced pan, in the oven about 10 minutes before you are ready to put the tart in. Place the tart tin on top of this and it will keep any overflow during the baking from messing up your oven.

This is the way I fill the tart case with the filling: I place the unfilled tart case in the oven on the pizza pan, then ladle the filling into the tart case slowly until it just reaches the top. This step saves you the trouble of having to then move the full tart case from the bench into the oven which invariably causes some spillage.

- Bake at 150°C for 35-40 minutes or until just set. Turn out onto a wooden board. Cool tart to room temperature. Dust with icing sugar. Garnish with candied orange (or candied lime) and decorative chocolates. Serve with double cream.

Henriques & Henriques, Sercial 15 years old, Madeira, Portugal

'What more complex wine than a Madeira to match the complex name Kama Sutra? Madeira is oxidative, nutty, smoky... A wine that is so versatile, can work as a predinner, during dinner, or after dinner. I prefer it with sweet, and chocolate makes the trick! Madeira wines are fully oxidised through years of exposure to humidity, sun light and oxygen.'

Carlos Simões Santos

Lemon Curd Cheesecake

lemon curd:

INGREDIENTS

180 g butter
¼ cup caster sugar
⅔ cup strained lemon juice
3 eggs

METHOD

- Put butter, sugar and lemon juice in small pan over low heat.
- Stir until butter is melted and sugar dissolved.
- Remove from heat and whisk in eggs. Stir over low heat continuously for 8-10 minutes until thickened.

This makes about two cups and even though the recipe only calls for one cup, I've found it better to have more around, than less.

base:

INGREDIENTS

175 g shortbread, or Marie biscuits, finely crushed in blender
¾ cup almond meal
75 g melted butter
1 cup lemon curd (see below)

filling:

INGREDIENTS

600 g soft cream cheese
½ cup sour cream
2 eggs
1 cup caster sugar
1 tsp vanilla extract (or split vanilla pod)

METHOD

- Preheat oven to 160°C.
- Combine biscuits, almond meal and butter.
- Press into base of 8 x 12 inch springform cake tin lined with baking paper.
- Put in refrigerator for a half hour. Mix or process cream cheese, sour cream, eggs, sugar and vanilla until smooth.
- Pour mixture over the base. Spoon lemon curd over the top and smooth out.
- Bake for 30 minutes or until set. Refrigerate until cool.

Pineapple Upside-Down Cake

INGREDIENTS
1 ⅓ cups all-purpose flour
¾ cup sugar
2 tsp baking powder
½ teaspoon salt
¼ cup vegetable oil
¾ cup milk
1 teaspoon vanilla
1 egg
grated rind of 1 lime
1 tbsp fresh lime juice
¼ cup butter
½ cup dark brown sugar
1 fresh, ripe pineapple, sliced, or one small can of pineapple slices
15 pecans

Either use a cast-iron skillet or a 10-inch cake pan.

METHOD

- Preheat the oven to 180°C.
- In a mixing bowl, sift together the flour, sugar, baking powder, and salt.
- Add the oil and milk to the bowl and beat for 1 minute.
- Add the vanilla, egg, lime rind, and lime juice, blending until just combined.
- In the pan or skillet, over medium heat, melt the butter.
- Remove from the heat and sprinkle the brown sugar around bottom.
- Arrange the pineapple slices and pecans over the sugar.
- Pour the batter evenly over the top.
- Bake for 45 minutes.
- Test for doneness with a satay stick or knife. If it comes out clean, it's done.
- Cool the cake in the pan for 5 minutes.
- Turn out onto a large serving plate.

Kahlua Pecan Pie

This is a classic pecan pie from the American south. You can substitute bourbon, brandy, rum, buttermilk, sour cream and chocolate chips, amongst other things. This one has a *Kahlua and brown sugar syrup*, added just before serving, which makes it very moist and puts it somewhere between a traditional pecan pie and a baklava. I tasted his variation a couple of decades ago, in Sebastopol, CA.

pasta frolla, 1-2-3 pie crust:

INGREDIENTS
105 g cake flour, sifted
105 g plain flour, sifted
140 g unsalted butter, cold
70 g caster sugar, or less
1 egg, beaten (optional)

METHOD
- Using a cheese grater, grate the cold butter into a large bowl. Cream butter and sugar lightly. Add the beaten egg and continue creaming until absorbed. Carefully fold in the flours, mixing only until just combined. The dough will still be a little sticky. Wrap in plastic wrap and chill for at least an hour. Remove dough from fridge and let rest for 15 minutes. Knead the chilled dough lightly first to soften, then roll out evenly in all directions, with a small amount of dusting powder, to about ⅛ inch in thickness.

blind bake:

- Preheat oven to 180°C. Line a 9-inch pie pan with the pastry, pressing gently into base and sides. Cut excess pastry around edge with rolling pin, cover with plastic wrap and chill the tart case for one hour. This will keep it from shrinking in the oven. Press a layer of aluminium foil into the pastry case and fill with beans or weights. Bake for 10-15 minutes. Remove from oven when outer edge of crust is light golden brown. Remove beans and check bottom. If bottom is still moist, return to oven (without beans) for five minutes until base is ready.

filling:

INGREDIENTS
3 large eggs
56 g unsalted butter melted
⅔ cup to 1½ cups of light corn syrup – dark syrup, if you prefer

1 tbsp of brown sugar
¼ - ½ cup of Kahlua (the secret ingredient!)
1 tsp vanilla extract
170 g pecan pieces
42 g pecan halves, enough to go around the edge
½ tsp salt (optional)

METHOD

- Preheat oven to 180°C. Beat eggs well in a large bowl. Add brown sugar, corn syrup, salt, melted butter, Kahlua and vanilla to eggs and mix well with a whisk. Sprinkle chopped pecans in the piecrust and slowly pour mixture over pecans. Decorate with the pecan halves around the outside edge. Bake on middle rack at 180°C. After 15 minutes, the filling should begin to set. Lower the heat a little and bake for an additional 15 -20 minutes, or until a wooden skewer poked into the centre comes out clean. Don't over bake. Remove from the oven and cool before serving.

Kahlua and brown sugar syrup:

- Put some light corn syrup, Kahlua and brown sugar into a saucepan and reduce gently by half. (Vary the ingredients to taste). Pour this over the whole pecan pie, or over each individual serving. Ice cream, or cream, on the side.

Good karma pudding

INGREDIENTS

Bolivian yak milk.
Zen wine, warmed over burning ghee-brushed cow patty.
Free-range fairy penguin eggs.
Hydroponic Cordovan blood orange.
Organic vanilla bean pod, dried for 24 hours,
on a Venezuelan Socialist's roof tile.
Biodynamically grown Australian Paperbark.
Cage-free echidna butter.

METHOD

Preheat a solar-powered, or bicycle-pedal driven, pizza oven to lowest temperature.

Combine penguin eggs, yak milk, blood orange rind and vanilla pod, in a small prayer bowl.

Whisk, non-violently folding-in, yin with yang.

Sit on South American embroidered cushion, for three days.

Non-destructively brush both sides of paperbark pieces

with echidna butter, place into a hand-thrown stone bowl,

into the oven, facing away from the door,

(being mindful of feng shui.)

Meditate 30 minutes.

Ring a prayer bell.

Bake until custard is firm.

Servir:

Place on a bed of shaved glacial ice, if desired, (although the goal is to be free from desire.) Serves one small carbon-footprint free village.

Wintermoon Persimmon Pie

Twenty years ago, I performed at the Wintermoon Festival, in Mackay, Queensland. Michelle Hartmann, from Shelley's Blue Tongues Wizards, was cutting what appeared to me to be a raw persimmon and eating it in slices. I asked her how she could stand them like that. She said this was a sweet non-astringent seedless variation that is actually better-eaten firm, rather than soft and squishy. I had a taste, and the idea came to me that they would probably be good in a pie, so I went into the Wintermoon festival kitchen, made sure the old oven worked, cranked up the gas bottle, assembled the ingredients (mis-en-place) and, in the narrow window of time, between a performance set, and a song writing workshop, I whipped it all together. It was very light and outstanding. Everyone who had a piece gave it a thumbs-up.

I should note, that up in Mackay, there were big boxes of persimmons all over the kitchen, gathered from a local orchard, but when I made this pie again back in Melbourne, a couple of days ago, I had to pay $1.20 per fruit! You don't miss your persimmon until your tree runs dry.

There are two types of persimmons grown in Australia: astringent, and sweet (non-astringent). Astringent persimmons need to be eaten very soft and are the only ones I had been familiar with previously. Sweet non-astringent persimmons are best eaten firm. The best varieties are Fuyu and Jiro and are available seeded or seedless. This recipe is made with the hard, seedless and sweet non-astringent variety.

INGREDIENTS
12-14 persimmons
80 g unsalted butter
¾ cup mixed sugars (caster, raw and brown)
1 tsp vanilla essence, or use a split pod if you prefer
1-2-3 short crust pastry (pasta frolla), enough for bottom and top
extra butter for basting top
icing sugar

pasta frolla, 1-2-3 shortcrust pastry:

Named thusly so as to make it easy to remember: 1 part sugar, 2 parts butter, 3 parts flour. This pastry freezes well and is so tasty that you can freeze the left-over bits and just roll them at a moment's notice into shortbread biscuits to quickly bake for ten minutes and have with tea or coffee.

Make sure the butter and the dough are cold when you work with them otherwise it becomes too icky and sticks to everything. I'm using raw sugar this time (instead of caster sugar) as it makes the texture is a little more al dente.

INGREDIENTS
1 egg
100 g raw sugar
200 g unsalted butter, chilled.
300 g plain flour

METHOD

- With a cheese grater, grate the cold butter into a bowl. Add sugar. Cream butter and sugar lightly. Add the egg and continue creaming until absorbed. Carefully fold in flour, mixing only until just combined. The dough will still be a little sticky. Divide into two sections, one slightly larger than the other, for the bottom crust and the top crust. Wrap in plastic wrap and chill for at least an hour. Knead the larger chilled dough lightly first to soften, then roll out evenly in all directions with a small amount of dusting powder. Not too thick.

Half blind bake:

- Oil and dust a pie tin and line with the pastry, pressing gently into base and sides. Cut excess pastry around edge, poke the base with a fork in a few places, so it can breathe, cover with plastic wrap and chill for one hour. Preheat oven to 180°C. Press a layer of aluminium foil into the pie casing and fill with beans or weights to keep the edges stable in the oven. Half-blind bake - just enough to firm it up - not enough to brown it - for 10 -15 minutes.

(Remember, you still want to be able to seal the top and bottom layers of the crusts.) Remove from oven. Remove beans and set bottom crust aside.

- Wash and peel persimmons with a potato peeler, removing caps (and seeds, if you use the seeded variety). Slice into thick apple-like slices. Melt the butter in a large pan and sauté the persimmons for about ten minutes. Add the vanilla essence and the sugars. Continue to turn and sauté as the sugar crystallises into a thick syrup. Don't cook the persimmons too long - keep them firm. Drain the syrup into a bowl and set the persimmon slices aside in another bowl. Return the syrup to the pan and reduce by half. Refrigerate both syrup and persimmons. While the persimmons and syrup are cooling, roll out the top crust pastry, the same way as the bottom. Not too thick.

- Fill the piecrust with the persimmon slices and top with the syrup. Dot small pieces of butter over the top and cover with the top crust. Pinch the rim so that the two crusts form a seal. Brush some melted butter over the top crust and poke in a few places with a fork to allow the steam to escape.

- Bake in a medium oven for about 20 minutes. Watch the crust. If the edges start to brown too fast, take the pie out of the oven and place a thin strip of aluminium foil around the edge to protect it and return to the oven until the top crust is uniformly light golden brown. Do not over bake. Cool the pie and dust with icing sugar. Serve with cream.

♪nOte: add some apple slices, sautéed in a little butter and sugar, for variation.

Mexican Peanut Butter Pie

crust:

INGREDIENTS

180 g digestive biscuits (Marie biscuits, or similar)
90 g unsalted butter
3 tsp caster sugar

inside:

1 cup thin cream
⅓ cup caster sugar
320 g cream cheese, chopped
375 g smooth or crunchy peanut butter

topping:

150 ml thick cream
150 g dark chocolate (70% solids), chopped
20 g unsalted butter
cocoa powder

METHOD

- Preheat oven to 160°C.
- Put biscuits in blender until fine crumbs.
- Add melted butter and sugar and blend.
- Press into base of 8-inch (22 cm) springform pan.
- Bake for ten minutes.
- Cool.
- Place cream and sugar in small saucepan and simmer over low heat for 4 minutes or until sugar dissolves. Blend cream cheese and peanut butter in blender. Spoon filling on pie crust. Cool.
- Bring cream to just below boiling over high heat. Remove pan from heat. Place chocolate in a tin bowl or heat-proof bowl. Pour the hot cream over the top. Leave for a few minutes without stirring. (Swish the dish around to merge chocolate and cream.)
- Pour topping over pie. Chill in fridge for 3-4 hours.
- Before serving, dust top with some cocoa powder.

Lemon Tart

Avere le mani di pastafrolle!
(To have shortcrust pastry hands!)

pasta frolla:

INGREDIENTS
1 egg (optional)
100 g sugar
200 g unsalted butter
300 g plain flour

METHOD

- Cream butter and sugar lightly. Add the egg and continue creaming until absorbed. Carefully fold in flour, mixing only until just combined. The dough will still be a little sticky. Wrap in plastic wrap and chill for at least an hour. Knead the chilled dough lightly first to soften, then roll out evenly in all directions with a small amount of dusting powder.

blind bake:

- Line a 3½ cm deep, 24 cm fluted tart tin, with a removable bottom, with the pastry, pressing gently into base and sides. Cut excess pastry around edge with rolling pin, cover with plastic wrap and chill the tart case for one hour. Preheat oven to 180°C. Press a layer of aluminium foil into the tart case and fill with pastry weights or dried beans to keep the edges stable in the oven. Bake for 10 -15 minutes. Remove from oven when outer edge of crust is golden brown. Remove beans and check bottom. If bottom is still moist, return to oven (without beans) for five minutes until base is ready.

lemon filling:

INGREDIENTS
3 large lemons
6 eggs
250 g caster sugar
200 ml cream
powdered sugar
extra cream for serving
candied orange and candied lemon peel for garnish.

METHOD

- Pre-heat oven to 160°C. Zest and juice lemons. Combine eggs and sugar until well-blended. Add zest and juice. Stir. Add cream and mix thoroughly using a whisk. Pour into just baked pastry.

- Bake for 35 minutes or until set. Cool in tin for 30 minutes before serving.
- Turn out onto a wooden board. Garnish with the candied fruit. Finding a whole candied orange isn't easy. I get mine from the local Italian deli. Cut the whole orange into thin slices and decorate the surface of the tart. You can alternate with candied lemon or lime for variety. Dust with icing sugar.

Mille Foglie

The grandmother of the Vanilla Slice.

INGREDIENTS

3 sheets 30 cm x 30 cm puff pastry
80 g caster sugar
450 ml cream
1 tsp lemon zest
350 g mascarpone
20 g icing sugar

METHOD

- Preheat oven to 200°C. Lay the puff pastry on a tray and prick well with a fork. This called docking and keeps it from expanding too much. Bake for 10-12 min or until golden.

(Tip: Puff pastry is better overcooked than undercooked.) Cool.

- Whip the cream, lemon zest and caster sugar until stiff peaks form. In a separate bowl, whip the mascarpone for 1-2 minutes until it firms a little then gently fold into the cream.
- Cut the cooled pastry sheet into 3 even pieces. On one piece of pastry, spread some of the cream mixture to a thickness of about 2 cm. Put another length of pastry on top and repeat reserving some of the cream. Put the third pastry sheet on top and gently press down.
- Using a flat knife, smooth the reserved cream over the sides and ends of the log. Dust the top lightly with icing sugar. Refrigerate for at least 2 hours before serving.
- To serve, slice carefully with a sharp serrated knife using a sawing motion. Stand the slices up on plates and serve with raspberry coulis.

(Optional: mound up some grapefruit and mango or any kind of fruit next to the slice and drizzle the coulis over.)

Raspberry Coulis

INGREDIENTS
2 cups frozen raspberries
2 tbsp caster sugar

METHOD

- Place frozen raspberries and sugar in a small saucepan.
- Bring to the boil, stirring and mashing with a wooden spoon, over medium heat.
- Simmer for one minute.
- Set aside to cool slightly.
- Press raspberries in a sieve over a jug to strain. Discard seeds.

Clafoutis

INGREDIENTS

300 g cherries
½ cup milk
½ cup cream
80 g sugar
3 eggs
seeds from ½ vanilla bean
pinch salt
200 g ground almonds
1 tsp flour
1 tbsp melted butter
1 tsp kirsch or Grand Marnier or Cointreau
zest of ½ lemon
1 tbsp sugar

short-crust pastry:

210 g flour, sifted
140 g unsalted butter, cold
70 g caster sugar, or less
1 egg, beaten (optional)

METHOD

- Using a cheese grater, grate the cold butter into a large bowl. Cream butter and sugar lightly. Add the beaten egg and continue creaming until absorbed. Carefully fold in the flours, mixing only until just combined. The dough will still be a little sticky. Wrap in plastic wrap and chill for at least an hour. Remove dough from fridge and let rest for 15 minutes.

- Knead the chilled dough lightly first to soften, then roll out evenly in all directions, with a small amount of dusting powder, to about an eighth inch in thickness.

blind bake:

- Preheat oven to 180°C. Line a 9-inch pie pan with the pastry, pressing gently into base and sides, (or use individual ramekins.) Cut excess pastry around edge with rolling pin, cover with plastic wrap and chill for one hour. This will keep it from shrinking in the oven. Press a layer of aluminium foil into the pastry case and fill with beans or weights. Bake for 10-15 minutes. Remove from oven when outer edge of crust is light golden brown. Remove beans and check bottom. If bottom is still moist, return to oven (without beans) for five minutes until base is ready.

- Halve and pit cherries. Place milk, cream, sugar, eggs, vanilla seeds and salt into blender and mix for one minute. Add the ground almonds and flour, followed by the melted butter, liqueur and lemon zest, and blend for one more minute. Leave the batter to rest for half an hour before using.

- Pour batter into a buttered shallow ceramic baking dish or partially baked 28 cm shortcrust pastry tart shell(s).

- Place the pitted cherries, about 1 cm apart, into the clafoutis. Bake at 180°C. After 15 minutes, the clafoutis should begin to set. Sprinkle the top of the tart with the sugar and return to the oven for 10-15 minutes or until properly set. It is ready when it's firm to the touch and light brown.

- To test, pierce the centre with a small knife; it should come out clean. Allow to cool to room temperature before serving as soon as possible with cream or ice-cream.

Red Velvet Cake w/ Cherries

Essere la ciliegina sulla TORTE.
(To be the icing on the cake.)

I don't need no smothered pork chops
I don't need no T-bone steak
just give me another portion
of that Red Velvet Cake

I don't need no crackling corn bread
I don't need no shake & bake
just give me some pecan frosting
on that Red Velvet Cake

*now don't slip in red food colouring
god knows we don't need a fake
just squeeze a little fresh beet juice
in the Red Velvet Cake*

*Sunrise is red in the morning
sunset is red on the lake
but there ain't no red half as red
as your Red Velvet Cake.*

Red Velvet Gold Coin & Snake Cake

A basic red velvet cake recipe with the addition of red snakes, tied with ribbons, between the layers and, in the old tradition, about fifty dollars-worth of gold coins scattered throughout.

cake:

INGREDIENTS
2 ¼ cups sifted flour
2 tsp cocoa powder
1 tsp baking soda
1 tsp baking powder
1 tsp salt
1 ½ cup sugar
75 g unsalted butter
2 eggs
1 cup buttermilk
60 ml organic red food colouring

(or, if you prefer, substitute beet juice, either from a can of pickled beets, or else boil up some beets, grate the boiled beets into the water, let steep for half hour and strain - or half beet juice and half food colour. This is a personal choice and, personally, I don't mind the food colour.)

INGREDIENTS
1 tsp white vinegar
1 tsp vanilla

frosting:

INGREDIENTS
240 g cream cheese
75 g unsalted butter
500 g icing sugar
1 tsp vanilla extract
1 cup chopped pecans

garnish:

INGREDIENTS
20 red snakes
20 green spearmint candy leaves
thin silk ribbon
50 dollars-worth of brand new one dollar coins
a creative little toy to decorate the cake as a centrepiece

METHOD

≡ Preheat oven to 180°C. Grease and flour two 9-inch round cake pans. In a medium bowl, sift the flour, cocoa, baking soda, baking powder, and salt together. Set aside. In a large bowl, cream sugar with butter. Beat in eggs, one at a time. Alternate adding flour with buttermilk to the creamed eggs and sugar mixture, stirring. Beat in the food colouring (or beet juice) and vinegar. Beat in the vanilla. Spread batter evenly in the pans. Bake 20 to 30 minute until a wooden toothpick inserted into the centre comes out clean. Turn out onto wire racks to cool.

- Wash and dry the gold coins. (I'm talking about Australian gold one dollar coins but anything will do. A mixture of one and two dollar coins. Depending on your budget: you could use *real* gold coins!)

- When the cake layers have totally cooled, place each cake layer on a separate cutting board to prepare. Gently push half the gold coins into each layer evenly so that each slice will contain one or more. Use a small knife if necessary to make it easier to insert the coins without damaging the cake.

- Tie a small bow around the neck of each red snake.

- Prepare frosting, in a large bowl, cream the cream cheese and butter. Beat in the icing sugar until fluffy. Beat in the vanilla. Stir in the pecans.

- Lay out the first cake layer on one of the cutting boards and put about a third of the frosting across the top and sides. We want to frost as much as the cake as possible before we add the snakes and put the layers together to avoid getting frosting on the snakes. Do the same with the second cake layer. Using two spatulas, gently and carefully lift the bottom layer onto a serving dish. Carefully place the red snakes evenly in a spoked wheel across the layer so the ribboned heads poke out from the sides about an inch or so. Push them gently into the frosting so that they stay in place.

- Carefully place the second cake layer on top of the first. Use the remaining frosting to fill in the gaps between the layers being careful once again not to get frosting on the snakes or ribbons. This requires concentration and focus. The heads of the snakes should cleanly poke through the frosted cake.

- Place the centre piece toy on top of the cake and place the green spearmint leaf candy around it evenly. If any of the coins are poking through, carefully clean the frosting away from the edges of the coins so that they gleam a little.

Watch the kids' faces when they see this and get their slice of red velvet cake with red snakes and coins. (Supervise them, parents, so they don't choke on either the ribbons or the coins.)

Red Velvet Cake w/Cherries

cake:

INGREDIENTS

2 ¼ cups sifted flour
2 tsp cocoa powder
1 tsp baking soda
1 tsp baking powder
1 tsp salt
1 ½ cup sugar
75 g unsalted butter
2 eggs
1 cup buttermilk
60 ml organic red food colouring (or, if you prefer, substitute beet juice)
1 tsp white vinegar
1 tsp vanilla

frosting:

INGREDIENTS

240 g cream cheese
75 g unsalted butter
500 g icing sugar
1 tsp vanilla extract
1 cup chopped pecans

garnish:

INGREDIENTS

Halved and sugared fresh cherries

METHOD

- Preheat oven to 180°C. Grease and flour two 9-inch round cake pans. In a medium bowl, sift the flour, cocoa, baking soda, baking powder, and salt together. Set aside. In a large bowl, cream sugar with butter. Beat in eggs, one at a time. Add the flour to the buttermilk, and then to the cream, eggs and sugar mixture, stirring. Beat in the food colouring (or beet juice) and vinegar. Beat in the vanilla. Spread batter evenly in the pans. Bake 20 to 30 minutes until a wooden toothpick inserted into the centre comes out clean. Turn out onto wire racks to cool.

- Prepare frosting, in a large bowl: cream the cream cheese and butter. Beat in the icing sugar until fluffy. Beat in the vanilla. Stir in the pecans. Use frosting to fill and frost the cake.

- Place halved and sugared fresh cherries for garnish.

Variation with pecans

acknowledgements

Pasqualina Brassachio Dolce (my grandmother) for my first introduction to incomparable world-class tail-to-toe cuisine – from growing to serving - at the earliest possible age; Grace Samartino Dolce (my mother), who had the unenviable task of living in the shadow of my grandmother's cooking genius. She worked a part-time job all her life to help my father support our family and didn't have the luxury of experimenting in the kitchen and garden daily, as grandma did, yet still was able to create vivid and memorable dishes for us kids; Lin van Hek (my everything), who taught me her precious goulash, which I have never been able to surpass. Her recipes were the first time I had ever eaten Lamb Shanks or Roast Pork with a perfect crackle. For decades, when our kids were small, she prepared every aspect of the food for our large family festival gatherings, on a grand and memorable scale;

Danielle Zanetti, our beautiful daughter-in-law, the Queen of Chocolate Cake, who has carried on the tradition of fine cooking for her own family (she taught our five-year old granddaughter, Misti, to make one of the best salad dressings I have ever had!); Annie Fiume, who contributed the Preserved Lemon recipe and has always been supportive of my cooking eccentricities. She once told me, 'You can cook anything'; Nguyễn Manh Chiến, one of my newest young friends, from Vietnam, now living in Australia, who taught me how to make his North Vietnamese salad and often fine-tunes my Vietnamese dishes with his own precise skills and memories of growing up with this spectacular cuisine his entire life; Carlos Simões Santos, Master Sommelier, at Vue de Monde, for his generous wine-food pairing of some of my recipes; and Loretta Sartori, for pretty much teaching me how to bake and generously empowering me, later on, in my own creations.

Don't trust books that talk about this art: for the most part they are misleading or incomprehensible especially the Italian ones; the French ones are not as bad – from one or another, you'll be able to glean some useful notion when you are already familiar with the art.

Pellegrino Artusi, the first writer to include recipes from all the different regions of Italy in a single book, **La Scienza in cucina e l'arte di maginare bene**. 1891.

Mangia!

about the author

Joe Dolce was born in 1947, in Painesville, Ohio, USA, moved to Australia in 1979 and is a dual National citizen of both countries. He is a song-writer, composer, performer, poet, film reviewer and essayist. He was a 2021 City of Melbourne Poet Laureate, Highly Commended in the 2020 ACU Poetry Prize, short-listed in the 2020 & 2014 Newcastle Poetry Prizes, short-listed in the 2019, 2018, 2017 & 2014 University of Canberra Vice-Chancellor's Poetry Prizes and awarded First Prize in the 2017 University of Canberra Vice-Chancellor's Health Poetry Prize, for his choral libretto, *And let the wonder in*. His poetry was included in Best Australian Poems 2015 & 2014 and he was winner of the 25th Launceston Poetry Cup (2010). He is the author of three books of poetry, the most recent, *At the Noisy Café*, published in 2023, by Busybird Publishing.

In the 90s, he composed and orchestrated an SATB oratorio, *Joan on Fire*, which was performed by the Melbourne Chamber Orchestra and Chorelation choir at the Melbourne Baptist Church. He taught Composition, Setting Poetry to Music, and Ensemble for two years at the Australian Institute of Music. He is more popularly known, internationally, for writing and performing the song, *Shaddap You Face* (1980-81) which was the Number One 45 rpm record (back in the days when they made 45 rpm records!) on the pop charts in a dozen countries and held the nine-times platinum award for the most successful song in Australian music history for four decades. He is co-writer, with Lin van Hek, of the song *Intimacy*, which was part of the soundtrack of the sci-fi masterpiece, *The Terminator*, selected as part of the United States Library of Congress National Film Registry archives. His songs have been recorded, internationally, by scores of artists. In 1981, he was presented with the Advance Australia Award by Sir Rupert James Hamer, AC, KCMG, ED, Premier of Victoria.

The recipe for *Basil-Chili Tomato Sauce, with Guanciale, Fennel Sausage & Kangaroo Braciole*, was the First Prize winner in the 2007 Hepburn Springs Swiss-Italian Festa Great Pasta Sauce Contest.

He lives in Carlton, Victoria, Australia, with his partner, of forty-three years, Lin van Hek.

www.joedolce.net

www.ingramcontent.com/pod-product-compliance
Lightning Source LLC
Chambersburg PA
CBHW051309110526
44590CB00031B/4357